MW00939650

Enjoy! Steve – I have been enjoying Piccadilly food since 1941

# cornbread

Sequel to Collard Greens with more memoirs about Growing Up on a Sandhill Subsistence Farm in Louisiana during the Great Depression

Thomas Ard Sylvest

**Thomas Ard Sylvest**

*AuthorHouse™*
*1663 Liberty Drive*
*Bloomington, IN 47403*
*www.authorhouse.com*
*Phone: 1-800-839-8640*



*Published by AuthorHouse 10/11/2012*

*ISBN: 978-1-4772-7857-4 (sc)*
*ISBN: 978-1-4772-7856-7 (e)*

*Library of Congress Control Number: 2012918743*



*This book is printed on acid-free paper.*

# Table of Contents

# INTRODUCTION

Cornbread and collard greens complement each other immensely when served together. So when a reader of *Collard Greens* asked me what my next book is going to be called I immediately replied, "*Cornbread.*"

*Cornbread,* then, appropriately becomes the title of this, my next book, sequel to *Collard Greens,* and features more stories about growing up on a sand hill subsistence farm near Provencal in Natchitoches Parish, Louisiana, during the Great Depression.

Europeans, upon arriving in the new world of the Western Hemisphere, particularly in the seventeenth and eighteenth centuries when our country was being formed, survived largely because their new acquaintances, the American Indians, shared a new cereal grain with them—corn, in the form of maize. They taught Europeans to survive by growing and learning how to preserve and process this new miracle cereal.

One episode, oft repeated, has a group of the newcomers stealing the winter supply and seed of the corn of their benefactors, incurring their ill will and putting themselves and their hosts at risk of starving.

Hoecake is a traditional North American dish prepared by mixing corn meal with a bit of fat and water and cooking the resulting paste on a flat, iron skillet. Sometimes it was even cooked on the blade of a hoe over a fire of wood coals, hence the name *hoecake*. It was used as a staple for feeding slaves, freemen, and masters across the South.

Reliance on corn for sustenance had not disappeared from the scene within the frame of time my memory spans as I entered the population surge in the southern United States at Provencal, Louisiana, in the third decade of the twentieth century. It was 1925, just before the beginning of the Great Depression.

Many is the time I heard my mother say to my father, upon his arriving home from a field late in the day, "Clean up and rest, sweetheart, while I make you a little hoecake."

So, lean back in your old cowhide-bottomed rocking chair, make yourself comfortable, and join me in the recounting of the times of the Great Depression in the hill country and Appalachian regions of our storied nation, not to exclude the remainder of the fifty states, as corn is a staple crop in the twenty-first century and is grown and consumed in all of them.

Corn, indeed, more than collard greens, characterized the basic staple food of the countryside of our country during the Great Depression.

Of the stories that describe the most memorable times of the Great Depression that are widespread and enduring, you will read a few representative ones in this volume.

One of the earliest memories I have of life on the sand hill farm at Provencal is that of crying to be permitted to accompany my father as he departed the house after lunch to return to work in the cornfield.

Minnie Fendlason Sylvest, my mother, told me that often she let me go with John D, my father, a few hundred yards to the edge of the cornfield when I was only a babe in arms to be seated on the ground at the end of the rows of the cornfield on a quilt, much to my delight. There I was happily entertained by the leaves on the stalks of corn waving in the breeze, only to scream with disappointment when I was forced to return indoors.

As an agriculturist by heritage and education, corn remains forever one of my favorite crops.

Evidence of the importance of corn to our culture is offered in the form of the twenty-first century laws which presently provide for the government's subsidizing of the growing of corn, even as I write this, by requiring that alcohol be incorporated into every gallon of fuel sold for fuel consumption. This is called *gasohol,* a mixture of alcohol, often from corn, and gasoline from petroleum. Often the subsidizing of one commodity results in an imbalance in the market forces and causes some other commodity to be priced out of the normal comparable ranges. When the price of corn is supported to induce growers to grow more for gasohol, the artificially high price leaves other consumers of corn paying abnormally high prices for corn to feed hogs and cattle, resulting in high relative prices for pork and beef. The ripple of this economic effect goes on and on.

After writing and publishing *Collard Greens,* I continued to write stories of my experiences growing up in Provencal during the Great Depression. They began to accumulate. I made the decision to save them for publication later.

*Cornbread,* this book, is the result.

# WHEN I WAS JUST A LITTLE BOY

When I was just a little boy,
I lived upon a farm.
As children, we would often play
In the hayloft of the barn.

In the hayloft of the barn, we'd play,
In the hayloft of the barn.

In the hayloft of the barn, we'd play,
In the hayloft of the barn.

The setting hen, she built her nest
In the fresh, sweet, new mown hay.
Now Mama said, "While you are at play,
Son, please go gather the eggs."

Now Mama said, "While you are at play,
Son, please go gather the eggs."

Now Mama said, "While you are at play,
Son, please go gather the eggs."

When it was time to milk the cow,
In the morning and at night,
"Bring me the bucket," Mama said.
"Son, I'll teach you how."

"Bring me the bucket," Mama said.
"Son, I'll teach you how."

"Bring me the bucket," Mama said,
"Son, I'll teach you how."

So, basic skills, my mama taught.
We had to learn them all.
You never know what you may need,
So you must learn them all.

You never knew what you may need,
So you must learn them all.

You never knew what you may need,
So you must learn them all.

Gather the eggs and milk the cow,
Feed the pigs and learn to plow.
Harness the mules, and salt the goats.
Split the wood and cut the oats.

Harness the mules, and salt the goats.
Split the wood and cut the oats.

Pick the collards; shell the peas.
Peel potatoes and make some cheese.
Churn the butter; make the bed.
Draw some water; clean under the shed.

Churn the butter; make the bed.
Draw some water; clean under the shed.

Churn the butter; make the bed.
Draw some water; clean under the shed.

Fix the roof down the hall.
Repair the gutter; don't play ball.
Catch a chicken; ring its neck.
Or cut off its head, what the heck!

Catch a chicken; ring its neck.
Or cut off its head, what the heck!

Catch a chicken; ring its neck.
Or cut off its head, what the heck!

Some chicken and dumplings we will make.
Some sausage and syrup cake.
Some cracklins and potatoes fry.
Some hog's headcheese and shoofly pie.

Some cracklins and potatoes fry.
Some hog's headcheese and shoofly pie.

Some cracklins and potatoes fry.
Some hog's headcheese and shoofly pie.

Gather the clothes before it rains,
Just make sure the gate is chained.
Put a bucket under that leak.
We'll fix that gutter late next week.

Put a bucket under that leak.
We'll fix that gutter late next week.

Put a bucket under that leak.
We'll fix that gutter late next week.

Shuck and shell the corn to go
To Henry's gristmill, don't you know?

Pick off the peanuts we must parch
And shell some corn for us to pop.

Pick off the peanuts we must parch
And shell some corn for us to pop.

Pick off the peanuts we must parch
And shell some corn for us to pop.

Grapple potatoes and snap the beans.
Pick the melons and turnip greens.
Cut the okra; butcher a pig.
Haul the spring water; give me a swig.

Cut the okra; butcher a pig.
Haul the spring water; give me a swig.

Cut the okra; butcher a pig.
Haul the spring water; give me a swig.

Slaughter a goat; share the meat,
For in the Depression it was hard to eat.
Share with the neighbors who share with you.
By the grace of God, we made it through.

Share with the neighbors who share with you.
By the grace of God, we made it through.

Share with the neighbors who share with you.
By the grace of God, we made it through.

By Thomas A. Sylvest
April 2, 2011

# CHAPTER 1
# Sylvests Move to Provencal

The story of the Sylvests in Provencal begins with John D Sylvest purchasing 160 acres of pine woods land from a man named Tarver. The land had a nominal house on it with a porch across the front facing the west.

This was located one mile west of the Leesville-Hagewood Highway, a dirt road graded to some extent and graveled in bad spots.

During the 1920s, the improvement of that road had begun with crews of contract workers hired to build up the roadbed with soil and clay to specified widths, elevations, and grades with drainage along the sides of the road.

Contractors are said to have been able to use prisoners for labor in addition to other hired hands. Fill was moved with slips pulled by mules and by horse-drawn graders.

Upon completion of the roadbed, gravel was hauled and dumped on the full length of the road. It was designated on the 1930s highway department road maps of Louisiana as an improved gravel road.

The numerical designation was LA Highway 39. Sometime after World War II, the numbering system of Louisiana highways was changed, and the road is now designated as LA Highway 117. The Sylvests shipped their furniture by Texas and Pacific Railway train from Pineville, Louisiana, to Provencal in 1923. The steam-powered train was the most common mode of transportation in use for moving households in the 1920s, having replaced the ox wagon and horse—and mule-drawn wagons that were the primary means of hauling and relocating until after the Civil War.

What an improvement!

John D hired a man with a team to haul the family and household goods six miles to the house (sawmill shack) called "the farmhouse."

As the story was told to me by my mother, the family arrived there two days ahead of their bedding and furniture. So, to find some comfort in which they could sleep on the floor was the first business on the agenda.

No real challenge to a family raised in the piney woods of Washington and Rapides parishes. They would just send the boys, Spurgeon, who was nine, Frank, eleven, and Vince, thirteen, into the woods nearby and let them gather enough pine straw, by the light of the moon, to make soft spots to lie down.

The boys charged into their task. Looking for piles of straw, which naturally occurs in pine forests by wind drifts, they were soon back.

Minnie, somewhat surprised with how soon they had returned with so much straw, accepted the blessing thankfully and prepared places for the little ones to sleep. The older ones made out the best they could.

Before daylight, the adults were awakened by something crawling on them. Managing to get very little sleep, it was rewarding to see the sun peeping through the pine trees on the nearby hillside. As soon as Minnie could see, she found that the crawling creatures were hog lice. The boys, being enterprising as the times called for, had stolen the bed of the hogs, hence the hog lice that infested all the clothes and bedding of the family. So, while wishing to devote time to completing the move when the wagon arrived hauling the furniture from the train depot, time out had to be taken to wash and boil all the clothes in which the lice were imbedded.

Thankfully, those creatures prefer hogs to humans, so getting rid of them was a temporary chore rapidly accomplished.

This story was often told by family members when the pine straw boys had grown up and could be the objects of riotous laughter and fun poking at the joke the hogs had pulled on them.

Of the 160 acres, only ten acres were cleared and in cultivation. With four girls and three boys—Dixie, Artie, Vince, Johnnie, Frankie, Spurgeon, and Pauline, in that order—the prospect of clearing more land of the timber and underbrush was an early order of business.

During those times, additional sons were considered assets, as their unpaid labor on a homestead could contribute more than it cost.

Mules were needed to provide the power for pulling a wagon, plowing, and saddle mounts. John D traded for one mule owned by a contractor on the highway. The mule was given the name of Pearl. She had the distinct markings of a Spanish mule bloodline, namely a dun body color with a dark stripe down her backbone and characteristic dark stripes of the same color on her legs. This was the result of breeding a mare to a Spanish jackass (jack). This produced a very tough offspring but one characterized as having a mean streak. That mean streak came out in Pearl as her objection to being ridden. She was too old to break to the saddle. So, she never was useful as a saddle mount.

After working with these creatures for all my growing up years, I concluded that these Spanish mules were just smarter than other mules.

Another acquisition was a brown mule with a light-colored nose, the offspring of what was called a Missouri jack and a mare. The mare had died when the offspring was born, so the owner, a turpentine crew worker, had raised the little mule on a bottle with cow's milk. She was very gentle, and we called her Jane. Known to be gentle and good under the saddle, these mules were the favorites of the region.

Basic equipment required to perform the work of the farm and provide for the essential needs of the family included the livestock, mules, cows, pigs, goats, and chickens. These were raised on the farm. However, to get started required procuring the female breeding stock of each species.

No farm at the time could exist without a dog, which provided security for the premises. The dog chased away strange creatures from predatory animals and unwelcomed unannounced people whose intentions were not known.

The family dog—half collie crossed with whatever father passed through during the night—named Fido, black all over with medium-length hair, was soon in place as security officer in charge.

Basic sheds were in place, so there were pens with fences to contain the limited livestock in the beginning.

Some goats were obtained from Mart Donaho, a neighbor who owned a flock.

A day or two day following the arrival of the family by train, the household goods arrived in Provencal. They were unloaded from the train and placed in the railroad storage building, part of the rail depot.

The third day, household goods and furniture reached the new homestead. John D had arranged for a man with a wagon to haul the stove and furniture. The essential wood cookstove was unloaded by the teamster and John D. After the stove was set in place in the kitchen, Vince helped John D connect it to the flue overhead with stovepipe so cooking could move from the fireplace to the cookstove.

Civilization had arrived on the northeast quarter of section 18 on a wagon trail portion of a branch of the Old Spanish Trail, El Camino Real, The Kings Highway, from the Red River to Texas. Eventually this portion of that trail was to become Sylvest Road.

I checked it out recently and found that the homesite in the twenty-first century has grown up again in pine trees and the other typical north Louisiana sand hill forest native species.

# CHAPTER 2
# A New Little Brother

Ready to enter my fifth summer, only four years old, I was led by a big sister into the bedroom west of the living room of our Provencal home to see my mother, Minnie Sylvest. I remember being shown a new baby by my mother and being told it was my little brother. That was April 22, 1930.

Always a chubby baby, and cute, Royce Elton Sylvest was to become my closest male member of the family. Ruth Germaine, our sister, had been born on May 15, 1927. She was busy trying to get to be three years old while I was working as hard as I knew how to get to be five.

Don't kid yourself: growing up out in the woods of Kisatchie National Forest was hard work, a full-time job for each of the three of us.

I do remember pulling Royce around in our red wagon that an older sister had bought for us. For the record, we called him Elton, his middle name, until he was grown. Uncle Sam, being no respecter of persons, couldn't care less about middle names, so when Royce Elton Sylvest joined the United States Navy, he immediately became Royce E. Sylvest and was called Royce for the rest of his life.

Before Royce was two years old, I started to school. I remember him sitting in a red high chair that John D had made. Royce was always pleasant and smiling. He must have been born with that great, generous, and pleasant personality, which he graciously displayed as long as he lived.

One day, in the summer of 1932, right after Royce had his second birthday, we had all had lunch and it was kind of quiet. As I recall, Ruth and I had been playing in the yard and had just walked into the house in the afternoon.

Mama said, "Where is Elton?"

We told her he had not been with us.

Panic! I remember everybody hollering and running everywhere looking for Elton.

We looked for his tracks. We called him.

No Royce. After all, where can a two-year-old go? It would be hard for him to open a gate and get out of the yard.

Not under the house, not in the smokehouse, not in the potato house. No more houses in the yard to look in.

We even looked in the well.

Everybody was praying, "Lord, help us find our baby boy."

With everyone looking, it took only about ten minutes to look in every spot, room, and corner on that farm, or so we thought.

Then somebody went to the barnyard, which we called the lot, to be sure he hadn't gone there and gotten in trouble with big farm animals: cows, pigs, mules, and goats.

Next, somebody was told to go to Henry McGaskey's house, a quarter mile away, to tell them so they could help look for Royce in case he had gotten out of the yard and walked away.

Suddenly somebody yelled, "Here he is!"

"Where?"

"He was asleep in the dirty clothes pile."

Yelling and hollering and telling everybody we had found him was a noisy time.

With prayers of thanksgiving and laughter all around, poor, little Royce was awakened from his nap, hugged, and pulled from one family member to the other, as if everyone had to touch him with their own hands to be sure he was real and was okay.

For me, that was one of my heaviest adrenalin days of my entire childhood.

I am still thankful that it turned out well.

We had a door in the main bedroom which, when opened, closed off a corner of the room. On the floor behind that door was where dirty clothes were thrown as they were accumulated preparatory to the weekly wash.

To a sleepy two-year-old, what could be a more comfortable place to take a nap? A big pile of clothes that smelled like all the people in the world that he loved was an ideal place to take time out for a nap.

Royce was never known for making bad judgments. He was a smart guy. I should know. He was my new little brother and remained that forever.

I loved him dearly.

Royce had an awesome musical voice, ear, and instrumental talent.

When he was in first grade in 1936, the elementary school faculty at Provencal school discovered his talent.

They decided to have a Tom Thumb Wedding, a miniature wedding of the first and second graders, and cast Royce as the groom.

That was one cute little kid in his tuxedo. The highlight of the wedding was Royce singing "I Love You Truly" on bended knee to his bride. This production was performed on the stage in the high school auditorium before the entire student body of Provencal High School.

I was one proud big brother and remained that way all my life.

I remember well that Royce was accompanied on the piano by Mrs. Hazel Hawthorne, the second grade teacher and a good musician.

Royce was the star of the show. The entire family was justifiably proud of him. I still miss him.

# CHAPTER 3
# Outhouses

The term *outhouse* might refer to any building on a piney woods homestead other than the home.

When I was a kid at Provencal, during the Great Depression, it referred to the outdoor toilet where one went to execute functions which are nowadays assigned to the bathroom. Not all of these functions took place in the outhouse. Sometimes containers were used indoors so the ladies, the elderly, the young children, and the ill would not have to make the trip outdoors in the dark, the rain, and the cold.

Some indoor arrangement was of extraordinary value and much appreciated when it was raining or cold or windy outside. Eventually the pit under the outhouse was the destination for sanitary disposal of household waste products.

An outhouse could be of many structural designs. Typically, they were small square buildings about six feet by six feet with a bench that had a hole cut in it. A pit was dug and the building, built on runners or slides, was pulled over the pit by a draft animal or two—horse or mule. With usage over time, the building would need to be moved to a new pit. The original pit would be abandoned and buried.

Location was a major consideration when building an outhouse. Good design dictated that it not be a major view when one approached the homestead. Sanitary concerns dictated that it not be on the uphill side of the residence and water source, the well or spring. The building was often screened with some shrubs, like ligustrum, so the building itself was not visible until you were within a few feet of it.

Inside the building, in addition to the toilet seat, were nails driven into the wall so one could hang a garment, coat, washcloth, or towel. Typically, several nails were available.

A bushel basket woven of wood was usually set in one corner where materials from old newspapers to corn cobs to a Sears catalog to be used for wiping were kept. Any sanitary vessels needed had to be brought from the house by the customer, such as a pan of water, wash cloth, soap, and towel.

Some outdoor toilets were larger and had a bench with more than one hole of different sizes so more than one person could carry out their functions simultaneously. This was useful to mothers with children during the potty-training stage and to family members who had difficulty with trots on occasion.

The typical outdoor toilet was made of unpainted lumber. Usually just a frame with rough, sawed, one-by-twelve-inch planks nailed on it constituted the whole design. One door was placed in one wall.

I recall that Vince, my oldest brother, returned home from Chicago about 1930, where he had just graduated from Coyne Electrical Institute after having studied electricity. He brought his bride with him, Florence Spiers. Our farmhouse was already filled with eight people. The new list was John D, my dad; Minnie, my mother; my brothers, Frankie and Spurgeon; my sister, Pauline; my younger sister, Ruth; a new baby brother, Royce Elton; and me. With Vince and Florence, the total became ten.

I recall that when Vince and Florence arrived, the one bedroom that offered the most privacy, a rare commodity in a sawmill shack in the 1930s, was surrendered to Vince and Florence. The master bedroom was for my father and mother. The rest of us slept in the other two bedrooms.

The point of my telling you about the occupants of the house at the time is that it sets the stage for the most awesome construction project of outdoor toilet building I witnessed during my seventeen years of residency in the piney woods from 1925 to 1942.

Vince, unable to get a job of any kind in Chicago or Louisiana, farmed on the family homestead, along with his brothers, which kept the entire group supplied with food grown on the farm.

As the old outdoor toilet was a "one-holer," Vince observed that, with little children, it was often needed by more than one household member at a time, for which a one-holer was inconvenient. Since he could not find a job and had to stay on the homestead, he had the time to solve the problem posed by the one-holer.

Vince decided to build a new outdoor toilet.

What could he use to build the toilet? Pine poles cut off the homestead forest was his choice. Selecting a supply of pine trees about six inches in diameter, he cut and peeled the bark from pine trees ten feet long.

The trees were cut with a two-man crosscut saw. They were peeled by a gooseneck hoe, which had had the gooseneck straightened in the farm blacksmith shop until the hoe blade looked like a scraper with a long handle on it. That described the pole peeler. Such peelers were used at the time by loggers who cut pine poles and sold them to buyers for eventual use by utility companies as poles for telephone and electrical lines and to timber brokers who sold them to construction material people for piling. The blades were usually sharpened by hand with the use of files. Sometimes they were sharpened on a foot-operated, circular grinding stone.

The pine poles for construction of the outhouse would be built into the rectangular, oblong log cabin, the basic building support for the walls. When the log pen structure was erected, the door opening was cut by use of the crosscut saw to make an opening six feet eight inches tall and thirty-six inches wide. Vince had scrapped up three one-inch-by-twelve-inch boards to use in fabricating the door shutter.

Smaller pine poles were cut and peeled for the rafters and lathe for the roof. Cypress boards were cut and rived from bolts of wood taken from sinker logs in a cypress brake about three miles from the homestead. A supply of these blocks of cypress wood was on hand on the place in anticipation of replacing the homestead roof.

Nails were those salvaged from the process of tearing down and salvaging the materials of a school at Bellwood, Louisiana, for which job my father had the contract with the local school board. On our piney woods farm, these secondhand nails met several needs. One need met was a nail for any purpose could be found in one of the numerous kegs of old nails saved from the old building. You only had to find the right-size nail and then straighten it with a hammer.

The new outdoor toilet was nearly complete. Vince had found enough dressed lumber somewhere to make the bench to go inside. His design was to be a "three-holer."

What a Cadillac, outdoor toilet on the old Sylvest homestead! Nothing less!

I watched in awe as Vince worked on some wooden hinges with which to attach the door to the structure. The portions of the hinges to be fastened to the door shutter were fashioned as follows:

Materials: two boards each two inches thick, eighteen inches long, and six inches wide.

## Procedure:

1. Draw a circle six inches in diameter at one end of each board.
2. At the center of the circle, bore a hole one inch in diameter.
3. Shape the board so the six-inch circle is intact by cutting the board once so that the result is a six-inch circle with a tapered handle on one side of the board, which is two inches thick at the end opposite the circle. This can be nailed to the door.
4. Three three-foot two-by-fours, when nailed to the door shutter boards, will hold the door boards together. They should be situated one in the center and the other two twelve inches from the ends of the door.

5. A hinge board will be mounted, one on the bottom of the top board and one on the bottom of the bottom board. Each so positioned that the holes in the hinge boards extend four inches beyond the edge of the door.

The portions of the hinges that were to be fastened to the two-inch doorframe were fashioned as follows:

Materials: two boards each two inches thick by eighteen inches long and six inches wide.

## Procedure:

1. Draw a one-inch circle in the center of the large round end of each board. Trim around the circle until the circle becomes a round extension of wood one inch in diameter and two inches long, extending from the end of each board.
2. Cut the board from four inches below the bottom of the one-inch post tapered to a point two inches from the back edge at the other end of the board. Nails can then be used to nail the board to doorframe.

These can be trimmed to a usable length to fit, each on the edge of the door. Position each so it will receive the holes in the hinges on the door shutter portions of the hinges. This is done by placing the door shutter in the door opening and securing it there temporarily. Then insert one hinge at a time into the hole of the other half of the hinge. When in the proper position, nail the upright half of the hinge to the doorframe. Repeat that procedure with the other half of the other hinge. Your door will swing freely.

Gravity will keep the door on the hinges.

I recall that when Vince finished with the door, the facility was considered ready for use.

When the door was opened or closed, it made a squeaking noise so everyone within hearing distance knew that the toilet was in use. The same noise would be heard when the customer reopened the door and left the facility. Thus, you could use the squeaking of the door to announce to all that the facility was available again. I never found out whether this squeaking was anticipated. It did make for interesting conversation, a favorite pastime during the Great Depression. I recall someone making the remark that someone was going to have to put some soap on those hinges so they would not make so much noise.

It is my belief that the soap lubrication never took place.

Some minor details. At one end of the bench was the smallest of three holes. Vince was considerate of children. He made a small step in front to the small hole so little people could reach the bench. The small hole was closer of the front edge also to fit the smaller dimensions of little ones.

I recall when Dr. Henry Harris, brother to Carl Harris, my brother-in-law, brought his bride to visit at the Sylvest homestead around 1938. Dr. Harris was so caught up with the novelty of the outdoor toilet that when his wife went to use it, he grabbed his camera and stood directly in front of the door and had someone creep up and fling the door open so he could take her picture seated on the bench.

Some quite extraordinary commotion ensued.

Being a small child, I was never afforded the opportunity to see any picture that resulted.

I remember thinking, as I watched Vince work at building the outdoor toilet, that I would always remember how to build a door with homemade wooden hinges.

Well, I do remember how to build a door with homemade wooden hinges. However, similar to my goat management skills that I learned and have, so far, found to be relatively unmarketable, so with the skill of building homemade wood hinges. I really have never found a market for my skill in building wooden hinges for such doors.

Maybe one day Hollywood will call before such awesome knowledge is lost to the ages.

Perhaps telling this tale is the closest I have come to marketing that skill.

# CHAPTER 4
# Chickens and Eggs

The contribution of the chickens to the subsistence of the Sylvest clan on the piney woods hill farm during the 1920s and 1930s cannot be overestimated.

At all times, Minnie Fendlason Sylvest, my mother, kept a flock of laying hens. Usually the flock consisted of about twenty adult hens plus about twenty other chickens of various ages.

The major purpose of the chickens was to produce eggs for all purposes: consumption, sale, and hatching for replacing the flock.

The adult chickens were kept in a "chicken house" at night. The chicken house was about ten feet by ten feet and was about eight feet tall. The walls were of four-inch boards with cracks left between the boards about a half inch wide. This crack allowed for plenty of air circulation during the warm and hot months of the year.

Inside the house were poles about two inches in diameter that were mounted on the walls and extended the ten feet to the other wall. These were placed in this manner as a perch for the chickens when they were asleep. Extending from the ground up to the poles was a ladder type ramp about six feet long that had slats about eight inches apart that the chickens could use to climb up to their roosting spots.

Most of the time, the door to the chicken house was left open at night. This left the chickens free to come down from the roost whenever they chose in the morning. It also allowed them to go to the roost for the night whenever they chose.

As the chickens had to be fed and watered daily, and as they were under the purview of Minnie, the children were exposed from birth to the arrangements for and activities of the chickens as the children followed their mother.

I remember asking my mother to let me spread the shelled corn for the chickens. It was fun to watch the chickens compete greedily for every grain of corn, pecking one grain, swallowing it whole, and racing to another grain to beat the other chickens to it.

Each day chickens were fed scraps from the table, chopped collard greens, and chopped onions from the garden. In addition, they were able to range freely about the barnyard and eat whatever leftovers they could find around the cattle corral, which we called a "lot," as in "feedlot."

Water was drawn from our well in our backyard, and a bucket of water was carried to the chicken yard and poured into a watering trough.

There were dozens of breeds of chickens that could be chosen for a poultry project of any kind. Minnie chose the brown Leghorn, a Mediterranean breed of chickens known for their excellent egg production. Her reason for doing this was that the chickens, being brown, were better camouflaged and less likely to be consumed by hawks.

The roosters of the brown Leghorn breed were beautiful, being colored in much the same pattern as today's gamecocks which are used in cockfighting. Their feathers have beautiful shades of red, brown, and black.

Competing roosters often fought for their harems of hens. And they were vicious in their fighting, often leaving their competitor bloodied and even dead. Their fighting provided much entertainment to Ruth, Elton, and me, the three youngest of the clan.

After the fighting, there existed a pecking order in the chicken yard. The dominant male ruled the place. All other males ran from him. The next most dominant male also chased all other males in the chicken yard except the dominant one. To us children, this was fun to observe. The chickens were much like the children. The older, stronger children usually had their way while their parents struggled to teach kindness, fair play, and sharing.

The dominant male rooster was the sire to most of the offspring produced in the barnyard. That was okay with the owner as the stronger bloodlines prevailed.

Two egg nests in the form of boxes were attached to the wall inside the henhouse. Most of the eggs laid by the dozen or so laying hens were laid in these nests. "Picking the eggs" from the nests and bringing them to the kitchen was a choice job for a child. We all vied for the assignment. The laying hens often stole away from the hen house and made a nest in the hayloft over the cattle pen called a lot. It was fun to climb into the hayloft to search for a hidden egg nest. Sometimes the hen built her nest in the peanut crib. They would choose any place they could hide and feel safe.

Sometimes they laid eggs in the feed troughs of the cattle, horses, and mules.

Eggs were as much a medium of exchange in the hills of the South during the Great Depression as was currency. For years, the standard exchange rate was established at the local grocery stores by the merchant agreeing to pay ten cents cash for a dozen eggs or give fifteen cents per dozen in purchases. This meant that fifteen eggs could be exchanged for a pound of coffee, the cash price of which was twenty cents.

Sometimes the farmer had a line of credit at the grocery and general merchandise store, which enabled the debtor to pay increments on his account by delivering eggs to the creditor at fifteen cents per dozen.

Our favorite store at the time belonged to Harry Hawthorne. From that store, a man could buy bread, candy, a plow point, a horse collar, or a saddle. Or he could buy a pair of shoes of several different kind or a pair of overalls. Further, that was where all the food we did not grow was purchased, particularly flour, lard, coffee, sugar, salt, and pepper. That was a store where a lady could buy material to make a dress. Or thread to use on her sewing machine, or a needle or a thimble. Matches with which to light a fire in a wood stove or fireplace were favorite items to purchase.

I met a son-in-law of JB Scarbrough who told me that JB took over ownership of that store after Harry Hawthorne and that upon JB's death AJ Scarbrough, one of my high school classmates became the owner.

Typically, any and all of the items purchased were put on a store credit account, and much of the repayment was by bartering eggs and sometimes chickens.

All of this value for eggs put a demand on the eggs and chickens, which competed with their being used for food. For this reason, chickens were a substantial contributor to our life and well-being.

In addition to providing eggs for barter and consumption, chickens provided meat for cooking. Rice and gravy was a staple item served on the Sylvest farm table. The most likely source for flavoring the gravy was a chicken fried, stewed, or baked. The most competitive meat otherwise was the pig. Pork, bacon, sausage, and ham provided another source of the gravy, second only to the chicken. Third in that order was the goat. Much kid meat was used to provide nutritious food for a family during the Great Depression.

This demand for meat made it desirable to grow some chickens other than the laying variety. Laying breeds produced little meat.

One of the popular meat breeds or multipurpose breeds at the time were the Rhode Island Reds. We sometimes grew this breed so we would have an inexpensive source of protein.

The business of hatching and raising baby chicks until they were grown was entertaining to us as children.

It was always exciting when Minnie announced that she was going to put eggs under a setting hen.

We learned early in life that a hen decides to quit laying eggs on occasion as she is urged by her hormones to reproduce the species. When a laying hen decides to set, she begins to cluck, an unmistakable sign that she is ready to set. Sometimes she will start setting on one or two eggs laid in a nest by some other chicken. If left completely to her natural instincts, she would be setting on a nest of about twenty eggs which she had laid herself.

It does not matter who laid the eggs. When the hen is ready to set, she will cover any eggs put under her. Duck eggs, imitation eggs, goose eggs, or whatever. One egg or two dozen eggs.

Minnie Sylvest knew her chickens. She regularly checked them by taking them in hand and feeling the width between the pelvic bones to see which hens were laying.

This sometimes required a little boy to feed the chickens in the chicken house, close the door, catch the hens which were supposed to be laying, and hand them to my mother one by one.

Woe to the hen that was not laying, if that was her assigned duty. She was likely to get traded to the Watkins peddler, Mr. Pete Holland, who came around biweekly and was willing to take a chicken in exchange for some perfumed Cashmere Bouquet soap or some other toiletry or kitchen merchandise.

In addition to the laying of eggs, some of the chickens were young hens called pullets and were replacements for those laying hens that were culled or got too old to produce enough eggs.

Young pullets could begin laying eggs when they were only six months old. Most were in full egg-laying mode before they were nine months old. After one full year of egg laying, they were in decline and before they were two years old would be replaced with pullets.

The young male chickens were called cockerels and only a choice few were selected to become the breeding sires of the next generation of chickens. The other males were fed until they got to broiler stage, about six weeks old, and they were butchered for table consumption a few at a time. Without electricity and accompanying refrigeration, we could not butcher many at one time, as we had no way of storing them.

The event of a setting hen brought delight to the younger members of the household in the 1920s and 1930s. Minnie announced it to the household during the general family discussion that took place during a meal.

All members of the household who were present at the homestead appeared at each meal at the dining room table. So, when comments were made about the setting hen, everyone knew when the eggs had been placed in the nest of the setting hen. Everyone knew as well that about twenty-seven days later, all the eggs under that hen would hatch, and each egg would produce one baby chicken called affectionately a "bitty."

When chicken eggs hatch, the resulting bitty is capable of walking within an hour. They do not have feathers yet but are covered with down which protects them until they can grow feathers which takes about two weeks. Their early growth rate is phenomenal.

As the bitties needed protection from all the hazards of the barnyard, such as getting stepped on by a mule or cow plus the threat of varmints like hawks and possums, my mother often had us take some boards from the farm scrap lumber pile, which was commonly found around any piney woods farm, and construct a pen about three by three feet for the hen and her babies. This pen was close to the house where my mother could monitor and protect the bitties until they were about two weeks old. By this time, they were ready to race after their mother all day, chasing insects, worms, and feed which we provided in abundance from the corncrib. We moved the pen back to the chicken yard before the bitties got used to being near the house and garden. In this way, the hen would be ready to introduce the broiler-size bitties to the chicken house and roost as soon as they were ready.

If the brood of bitties hatched out in the wintertime, which was sometimes the case, Minnie took the baby chickens into the house in a cardboard box deep enough so they could not hop out of it—about twelve inches deep. That box was kept indoors for several days until the baby chicks could be expected to be well protected by their mother hen. This was usually after the chicks were about a week old.

It was not necessary for the bitties to be placed back with the hen. Usually they were, but they could be raised by hand in their own enclosure and returned to the chicken yard when we chose, as we sometimes did.

Minnie knew how to get little chicks off to a good start. Typically, they were fed on boiled eggs for about the first three or four days. Then they were graduated to crumbled cornbread and leftovers from the table, such as cereal, vegetables, and scraps.

After about six weeks, they were ready for their primary diet of shelled corn supplemented by the table scraps and greens from the garden. Some of the things we fed to them were boiled or baked sweet potatoes. Other times we had a milk cow that had recently calved and the abundance of that milk supply would be almost the complete diet of the bitties for a week or more.

Eggs from our laying hens were regularly used to exchange for any need of the family which otherwise might have been met with cash. Other chickens were produced with the goal of using them to trade and consume. They met this goal admirably.

As you can imagine, eggs to set under a hen were often exchanged with our neighbors. Sometimes a neighbor would send a child to borrow two eggs because her mother wanted to make a cake and had no eggs.

I recall Minnie taking me along with her as she walked a mile or two to a neighbor's house to cull their laying flock by identifying the ones producing eggs. This skill, and many others she and John D Sylvest, my dad, had learned from the LSU Agricultural Extension Service, an agency of the Louisiana State University in cooperation with the parish and state governments.

My parents had great respect for this service and often attended short courses, taught by the county agents, to learn new skills in raising a family on the poor soil of the piney woods.

The knowledge required to raise chickens for egg and meat production was a key to successfully providing for a growing family on a subsistence hill farm in the piney woods of the Great Depression.

I still like fresh eggs for breakfast.

# CHAPTER 5
# A "Collard Greens and Cornbread" Kind of Neighbor

We had some good neighbors at Provencal. One case that demonstrates the fact, indisputably, took place one summer day when I, a ten-year-old, was splitting stove wood in the wood yard back of the house.

Minnie called me and said, "Ard, (my middle name by which I was called as a child) run to the field and tell John D and Mr. Kay that Mr. Kay's dogs are chasing our goats."

Mr. Kay was one of our closest neighbors. Mr. Pink and Mrs. Lottie Kay lived just north of us one and a half miles across the woods. This day, he was working in the field with John D, my dad, on some field project.

I was amazed that my mother knew that the dogs chasing our goats were indeed Mr. Kay's dogs, as the goats were a quarter mile away in the woods. She had heard the bleating cry of the distressed goat, the barking of the dogs, the ringing of the goat bell, and knew what was taking place.

When she told me to run to the field, she meant it literally, because it was an emergency.

I remember that Mr. Kay did not run, but he sure walked fast. I had to run to keep up with him as he hurried to the scene where the dogs were barking.

Two dogs were involved. Mr. Kay had an old faithful hog and yard dog named Jack. Everybody for miles around knew the names of their neighbors' favorite dogs if the dogs had any seniority at all. Jack had the reputation of being the best hog dog for miles around. However, Jack had the habit of handling pigs so roughly that he killed them. Mr. Kay did not want to give up his champion hog dog, but he wasn't going to let that dog kill pigs. To control that activity, Mr. Kay had taken his pliers and removed Jack's teeth. Jack continued to be the best hog dog in those woods for years.

As Jack was getting old, Mr. Kay had a young dog, about two years old, that he was grooming and training to be a good hog dog and a replacement for Jack when Jack's days were over. This young dog was white with black spots and, indeed, had been named Spot. Spot was fast. Could that dog run! Could that dog catch a hog! He was fast. And he had a great nose, that is, he could smell a hog and follow its trail. Even though Spot was a young dog, the whole neighborhood was aware that Spot was on his way to becoming a first-rate hog dog worth two months of pay in anybody's book.

When Mr. Kay and I got to the goats and the dogs, we saw that Jack had one goat hemmed into a corner. Jack was in her face, keeping her from running away, while Spot was ripping her apart from behind.

Mr. Kay, a big man, well over six feet tall and strong, to my total surprise and shock, reached down and grabbed Spot with one hand by both hind legs, lifted him up, walked about ten feet holding him up with his left hand, picked up a pine knot with his right hand, hit that dog three times back of the head, killing him instantly. He dropped that dog on the ground, dead. As he turned to walk away, Mr. Kay said, "I'm not raising any goat-killing dogs."

I was astounded. My eyes must have been as big as saucers. I could not believe that Mr. Kay had killed his own dog.

A lifetime lesson for me, a ten-year-old boy: your neighbor's respect and your respect for your neighbor's property are more important than your own dog.

I don't mind telling you right now that I never forgot that lesson; it is indelibly stamped into my brain. If you are committed to being a good neighbor, it is not a halfway thing. It is total.

You could not have a better neighbor than P. G. Kay, a real collard greens kind of a guy if there ever was one.

Mr. Kay died from cancer about two years later. I remembered, and I cried.

I still remember.

# CHAPTER 6
# McGaskey's Gristmill

In early 2010, I was on the telephone talking to Bertha McGaskey Ellis, youngest daughter of Henry McGaskey, who owned the gristmill near Provencal, Louisiana, to which I took corn to be ground each Saturday in the 1930s.

The lively conversation had gone on for some time when Bertha, nostalgically, said, "I sure wish I had a picture of my daddy's gristmill, but I don't know anyone who has one."

Time switched to reverse for me and quickly placed me in 1938 on a Saturday morning, sitting on a board bench near the gristmill.

The structure of the mill makes such a good backdrop against which to prop the images of the people Bertha would have seen in a picture taken that day.

Ellis Honeycutt was there waiting for Henry to crank up the engine and get the stone mill turning to make the staple item in our diet: cornmeal for cornbread.

Oscar, grown son of Henry McGaskey, who lived nearby, came under the tin mill shed on the east end and walked over to the front of the four-cylinder Model A Ford engine. A hand crank was in his hand. Inserting the crank into the slot, he stepped back for a minute, reached to the steering column, and reset the spark lever to facilitate combustion. Only then did he turn the crank with a mighty motion of an arm grown ever so muscular from years of hard, heavy work. As the engine coughed, caught, then raced into motion, Oscar reached back and relocated the spark lever to its original position.

Thirteen years old at the time, this piney woods kid looked with awe at the operation. How could Oscar have learned how to do all those magic tricks with that old engine? After all, only the chassis of the old car was there: no wheels, no body, no superstructure, and no seats. It looked to me like every part of the old car that could possibly have been removed was missing, Yet Oscar could walk up to that chassis, press a few parts to see that they were not about to fall off, pull that spark lever, put the transmission in neutral, grab that crank, and create an unforgettable spectacle of power, action, and sound with one mighty heave of his good right arm.

The chassis rested on four blocks of post oak wood, each about sixteen inches in diameter, which had been cut as posts and planted in the ground with the aid of a pair of scissor-action post-hole diggers. The blocks were about thirty inches tall and held the old Ford chassis steady as the drive shaft revolutions increased to mill turning speed and the millstones rubbing their rough scrolls together added their rumbling sound to the already deafening roar. One thing that old car did not have was a good muffler system.

So, everyone tried to ignore the noise and just yelled to be heard.

Water began pouring out of a pipe above an old fifty-five-gallon drum set on a post rack put there for that purpose. I studied that arrangement for a while and concluded that, since the engine did not have a radiator, the water pump recirculated the water from the barrel through the engine block, keeping the engine cooled to a safe operating temperature. No temperature gauge needed.

Oscar set the throttle handle in the remnant of a dashboard with his right hand, pressed the clutch in with his left hand, and shifted from neutral into low gear with his right. As the shift lever moved to a higher gear and the gears and pulley slowly began to turn faster the RPMs increased, audible to all ears, Oscar pressed the clutch again and shoved the shift lever to the upper right into second gear, where it was to stay while pulling the load of the stone mill. The decibel level rose until the grinding and screaming of all mechanisms drowned out the sound of all voices. Shouting into each other's ears became the norm for all vocal communication.

Studying the setup further, I observed that there was a belt pulley on the end of the drive shaft from which the differential had been removed. A heavy belt about ten inches wide rotated around the drive shaft pulley and traveled thirty feet to the bottom of the mill stone rack under which a larger pulley sat upright but on an angle of ninety degrees from the other. At a point halfway between the pulleys, there was an idler over which the moving belt moved, guiding it from the horizontal drive shaft to the vertical shaft of the mill.

I could feel the heat from the engine when at that end of the forty-foot shed and the warmness of the cornmeal dust as it filled the air around the mill at the other end of the shed.

At the mill end of the shed was the extended tin roof, which provided a shelter from rain and a place to get out of the sun in the morning when the sun was from the east. This was the nearest thing to a motor company waiting room that the 1930s had to offer out in the piney woods.

Anything with corn in it was either on a high shelf or in heavy containers as hogs ranged freely around the vicinity. A heavy board fence about three feet tall surrounded the mill frame, forming a yard of about fifteen-foot dimensions. The hogs were no problem when grinding day came, as the family dogs maintained dominance around their masters, which translated into, "No hogs allowed today."

There were occasional confrontations between canines that traveled faithfully with their head of households and were always ready to defend their masters to the death.

"Shut up, dog," was heard from time to time.

A bench of heavy planking, two-by-twelve, was sometimes filled with waiting customers and other times filled with sacks of corn or meal.

This was clearly a first-come, first-served process. This kid was not disappointed to discover, upon arrival at the mill that morning, that there were three people ahead of him. That meant that I would get to watch all these interesting operations, listen to the conversation of the community elders, and not be expected to arrive home until my sack of corn was ground and the resulting meal safely resided in the old lard can, which held about fifty pounds of cornmeal and sat at the end of the table in our kitchen.

I remember when I was five years old that I tried to climb upon that can, the lid was not securely on the can, and I fell into the can, hitting my front teeth on the edge of the can and knocking out one of my baby teeth. I was to start to school with that snaggle-tooth look.

Mr. McGaskey was a community fixture. Fair to all and generous, perhaps to a fault, he served all comers with grace. He knew every person in the community for miles around, and everybody knew him.

As each customer arrived with his bag of corn, Henry met him, told him how many customers were ahead of him, and placed the corn of the new arrival in the proper location. Sometimes a customer who lived nearby would make arrangements to leave his corn to be ground and would return a few hours later to retrieve it.

After agreeing with the new customer as to how much corn he had brought, a toll was taken from the bag of corn equal to one-eighth of the total. From a bushel of corn, that meant one gallon of corn was taken as toll. On a shelf about three feet off the ground adjacent to the millstones was a large wooden box. In this McGaskey kept his toll corn.

When corn is ground, the volume of the product meal is greater than the original volume of the corn. However, after the toll portion of one-eighth part was removed from the corn, the meal that resulted exactly equaled the volume of the original corn.

I was intrigued by the fact that the measuring box was a Brown's Mule Tobacco box. What made this even more interesting to me was the fact that my father chewed Brown's Mule Tobacco.

Can you believe? This outing to get corn ground on Saturday was a significant contact with the rest of civilization for this thirteen-year-old.

Mr. McGaskey loudly announced, "Next," which alerted me to the fact that my bag of corn meal was ready. With some regrets that my holiday-like interim at the mill was ending, I went over to the picket fence around the McGaskey garden where I had tied Jane, our most gentle plow mule and erstwhile saddle mount. I led her back to the mill where Mr. Ellis Honeycutt, a neighbor and friend, said, "Let me help you with that bag, son." Whereupon, he grabbed me, threw me up on the back of my favorite mule behind the bag of meal, and said, "Tell the folks hello, and I'll see you here next Saturday."

Who could ever forget such royal entertainment during his growing up years? Not me. With regrets that my Saturday adventure at the gristmill was about to end, I rode slowly back to the Sylvest homestead one-quarter of a mile up the road as the delightful roar and rumble of the engine and mill gradually faded into a distant hum.

Willie Foshee, standing nearby, said, "Come see us, son." Nearly all grown neighbors called their neighbors' sons "son."

It should not be assumed that the gristmill, equipment, and personnel were infallible. However, there was that atmosphere of dedication to service that would be the envy of any modern business.

One week during the summer of 1938, the old four-cylinder gasoline engine of the former Model A Ford that normally powered the gristmill gave out. Oscar announced that the mill could not run until the engine was overhauled. This word was passed around the community.

Henry McGaskey knew what to do. He contacted Ernest Bell, the school bus driver for our route, and arranged for Mr. Bell to come help him grind the corn that Saturday.

To my utter surprise, when I arrived at the gristmill with the Sylvest corn, the customers were there as usual and the gristmill was running. Not the usual dependable Model A engine but the school bus. Oh, my goodness! How can you turn a gristmill with a school bus?

Mr. Bell had backed the school bus up to within about forty feet of the mill. Instead of the belt being on the pulley of the Model A engine, the belt was put over the rear dual wheels of the school bus as the corner of the bus was jacked up and chocks put under the wheels on the other side of the bus.

Mr. Bell and Mr. McGaskey adjusted the position of the bus so the belt length just fit their needs. Transmission of the bus in neutral, the belt was put on the wheels and on the pulley of the stone mill. The engine was cranked and the dual wheels were set on low gear. The wheels turned. The belt went around, and then the mill began to rumble.

Hey, we'd have a grinding day at the McGaskey gristmill today just like on other Saturdays. Sure enough, we did. This is one of the episodes which I document to show how we learned to improvise during the Great Depression, an essential skill for the winning of World War II.

The stones of the mill were about thirty-six inches in diameter. About once a year, the stones had to be sharpened. This was a job that called for a skill of my dad. With his blacksmith shop hammer and a concrete gouge about an inch in diameter, John D Sylvest scoured out the design of the flutes on the grinding stones so their surfaces would have the necessary roughness and flute depth and design through which the ground corn would migrate to the exhaust spout as the mill turned.

This sharpening process would require most of a day, but the time required to grind a bushel of corn after the stones were freshly sharpened was reduced by almost one-half.

I wondered if I would have to learn to sharpen grinding stones of mills in order to earn a living.

Well, to answer your question, my life did not turn out that way.

Now I have shared with Bertha Ellis the only picture of her dad's gristmill that I know of. Bertha, enjoy! And may you not be the only reader who finds this description of your father's gristmill an enjoyable memoir.

Other heads of households I frequently saw at the mill with corn to grind in the 1930s were John Foshee, Elzee Honeycutt, George Sharp, Wiley Nabors, Henry Lynch, P. G. Kay, Myrtie Longino, Loy Montgomery, Ivey Honeycutt, Jefferson Masters, Dred Smith, Henry Lynch, and others I don't remember, plus many others whose names I did not know. Sometimes, other members of the families named made the trip to the gristmill:, a son, son-in-law, or grandson.

It was commonplace for multiple generations of a family to live together in the 1930s, as life expectancy was a few decades less than it is in the twenty-first century and living together was necessary to survive.

Going to the gristmill on Saturday was my favorite social event of the week next to attending church.

# CHAPTER 7
# Managing for Food Daily

The things that my parents and their neighbors did to keep food on the table through all the seasons of the year without refrigeration were almost endless in number and without ceasing from day to day. Every single day was set against the backdrop of "What step is next that will sustain our food availability?"

For some reason, both of my parents seemed to have a better handle on that concept than the typical piney woods resident.

The managing of the larder and the projecting of the needs of each category of food seemed to fall to my mother, Minnie Fendlason. She had the full support of my dad, John D, but it was she who concentrated on reexamining the elements which had to be combined to get the desired results six months down the road. They discussed the components that made up this total supply almost daily.

The hitching post foundation around which Minnie and John D built their annual plan was corn. Cornbread, the basic cereal, represented the staff of life on the Sylvest farm and was consumed daily. When the money was available to purchase wheat flour, it was used along with corn to make bread for daily human consumption. When available, flour was used to make biscuits for the breakfast meal with cornbread consumed at the other meals.

Each year the goal was to plant enough corn to produce an amount large enough to make cornbread for fifty-two weeks. While our goal was to have an abundant supply which made the managing of it easier, sometimes we would fall far short of that abundance.

A good year of corn production for us would require planting from ten to fifteen acres of corn. This would result in a production of from one hundred to two hundred bushels. This total was divided by twelve to arrive at the amount we could use each month. That amount was prioritized. First, for human consumption as cornbread; second, for the mules, our only source of power; and third, for hogs, which were our primary sources of meat.

In addition to the basic element, corn, the essentials were used as foundations for planning. It would not have occurred to Minnie Sylvest to have her family run out of a milk supply by not having a milk cow producing milk every month of the year. I do not remember a single time during my eighteen years under her supervision that the household did not have at least one cow giving milk. A milking cow was an essential, as there was absolutely no alternative source of milk. We had several milking cows most of the time.

Sometimes our surplus milk was such that we fed some to the chickens and pigs.

Laying hens were the second essential, as eggs were needed for balancing the diet and for barter for necessary purchases at the general store where we bought coffee, tobacco, kerosene, and matches.

The third essential was meat of animals as a source of fat and protein to add to that provided by milk and eggs. The basic source of fat was hogs, which we grew from baby pigs. Sugar-cured meat from the hog was the number one source of meat, which provided fat and protein. Lard rendered from the fat of butchered hogs provided shortening for frying and baking.

An additional source of fat and protein on our farm was goats. Highly nutritious, kid meat, the meat of young goats, is tasty and versatile. Like chicken, it can be cooked into stews, soups, and roasts.

Sometimes we mixed ground meat from kid and pork to make a special sausage which we preserved by smoking in lieu of the virtually unknown refrigeration.

Around these essentials were added all the other food items that could be grown on the farm.

It was about 1941 before electricity reached Provencal, still five miles away from the Sylvest homestead. At the time electricity arrived, the opportunity was present for a refrigerated food freezer to be erected at the school in Provencal with compartments for rent to members of the community. This structure was called the "Food Locker" and rapidly became popular for those who had a cash income with which to pay the monthly rent. Even though the rent was moderate, cash income was essential to pay the rent. The food locker was government owned and had been designed and promoted by the USDA.

Syrup produced from sugarcane which we grew was basic, so were potatoes, sweet potatoes, peanuts, and garden plants and fruit trees of all kinds.

Before trying to name all of these fruits and vegetables and the sources of each, we should look at the apportioning method being used, the real secret to our never being without enough food for the day.

Divide the corn into twelve equal imaginary amounts. Realize that there will be no more corn produced for twelve months so you cannot fudge. Much of our total supply of corn would go for making corn meal, from one and one-half pecks to two and one-half pecks, usually two pecks (one-half bushel) per week. One-half bushel per week means that twenty-five bushels of the year's supply is required for family bread.

An equal amount was required to fatten enough hogs to provide the rendered fat for lard. That would account for twenty-five more bushels.

Third, corn was required to feed the mules for a year. There went another twenty-five bushels.

Some corn had to be used to feed the chickens, as we could not do without eggs. We monitored this consumption closely as corn harvest time was months away, after we put this year's crop production in the corncrib in October.

Clearly, the means for procuring all of these fell naturally into two categories: plants and animals. These were closely related, as we saw above that without corn, there would be no hog. No hogs would mean no fat and no bacon, ham, or sausage.

When the subject up for consideration was whether we could butcher a certain hog, it was automatic that the considerations were the following: If we kill this hog, do we have enough hogs to produce the additional pigs needed in the future? Is the subject hog fat enough? If not, how long will it take to fatten it? If we have to fatten it, can we afford the amount of corn required without disfurnishing ourselves of the corn required for other purposes?

Similar considerations had to be given attention with respect to each of the other farm enterprises.

Even if we were considering cooking a batch of dried butter beans for a meal, we had to be sure we had put aside enough of that variety of beans to use for seed in growing more beans. The identical consideration had to be applied to all varieties of beans, peas, and other crops.

Even when it came time to plant them, we had to be sure not to plant all of the seed at one time in the event that the ones planted did not grow due to drought, flood, or any other cause and thereby deprive us of our final supply of seed.

As a major portion of our preserved food was kept in fruit jars, much effort went into the canning of foods, which was of such importance that it must be treated as a major subject of its own.

Makes me hungry for some of Algy Foshee's preserved pears right now!

## *Spring Food*

Each season on the Sylvest sand hill farm brought its own challenges. Springtime offered the opportunity to plant anew many of the garden and field crop plants that do not grow in the winter.

By the end of March, we were beginning to consume the last half of our corn crop. So, we monitored the decline of the corn supply in the corncrib closely.

Our corncrib was five feet off the ground and you could enter it only by climbing a ladder, which did not go all the way to the ground.

By the time I was fourteen years old, in 1939, I was the oldest child at home, the seven older ones having departed for higher education or occupations elsewhere. Being the oldest child at home, I was the one to climb into the crib and assess the supply of corn weekly, remove the determined amount and feed the mules each day, shell about a half gallon and feed the chickens each day, and shell the half bushel on Saturday and take it to the gristmill to be ground into corn meal.

Having an adequate supply to last until the new crop of corn matured and was harvested was such a critical need that I remember my mother coming to the front of the corncrib and asking me how much corn was left. Having no way to measure the amount, I gave her my best guess. Her concern was apparent as she came to the ladder and climbed up about three steps until she could see the size of the pile of corn on the crib floor. Satisfied with that evaluation, she used that information to guide me in how much corn was to be used each day and week for each purpose.

The 1939 cornfield had been planted during the last week of February and the first two weeks of March. We could consider planting a bit more as March was just ending.

Cane had been planted, and by March 22, the first day of spring, the cane was a foot tall.

We were assured of a good stand of cane, which augured well for a good crop of cane syrup to be made in the fall for the following year.

We still had turnips, collards, cabbage, beets, and onions growing in the garden. We were relying on these plants to keep us supplied with fresh vegetables for the table. They were our main source of vitamins. Yes, by 1939, several vitamins had been discovered and my parents were keenly aware of the need to provide children and farm animals with nutritionally balanced nourishment. This included plenty of green vegetables. As a growing child, I recall taking cod liver oil, a good source of vitamin D essential to prevent rickets. And rickets were not unknown among the children of the Depression in the piney woods of the South.

The calcium needed to go with the vitamin D was abundant in milk, which we always had and usually in abundance.

The supply of sugar-cured pork in the form of bacon, hams, and shoulders was holding out well. We consumed some daily for breakfast and some at other meals on occasion.

Breakfast usually included biscuits, bacon, fried eggs, cane syrup, milk cream, and butter. Sometimes canned, preserved fruit was placed on the table as a sweet alternative to syrup. This could include preserves or jam made of blackberries, blueberries that we called huckleberries, peaches, pears, plums, apples, or strawberries. Usually these were in quart jars, but sometimes they were in gallon jugs.

As the season moved on into April with milder temperatures, preparation for the planting of more vegetables began. By the end of April, we had English peas from the garden to add to our available vegetables. Beans and peas of other varieties were in the process of being planted.

We were flat looking forward to the new vegetables that would soon fill our table with a variety. Fresh tomatoes, field peas, green beans, butter beans, squash, eggplants, sweet peppers, hot peppers, cucumbers, cantaloupes, and watermelons would be coming into season as summer wore on.

We canned many of the above as they became available.

In late summer and early fall, August through October, fruit of all kind became ripe and canning took place as the various fruits matured.

Never were we without an abundance of okra in season. That was from about June 1 to October 1. We canned it mixed with tomatoes, which are harvested during the warm and hot months like the okra.

I can remember ten one-gallon glass jars of tomatoes sitting in the corner of our dining room right after we had completed the tomato canning. All of these canned goods had to be protected from freezing. That we usually did by keeping them in the kitchen, which had a fireplace or the dining room adjacent.

We would have several periods of freezing weather every winter. Sometimes the temperature would be below freezing for only one or two nights in a row with temperatures rising to above freezing during the day.

On a few occasions, the temperatures would stay below freezing for more than forty-eight hours. That we regarded as a severe cold spell in Natchitoches Parish.

I remember on a few occasions that we had a few jars crack during a freeze. When that happened, we took emergency precautions immediately to protect all of our remaining canned goods.

Keeping a wood fire burning in the kitchen fireplace all night was an option we used more than once during hard freezes when I was growing up. Keeping a wood fire burning in the wood stove in the kitchen was also an option we sometimes used. Either required modifying your sleep pattern to stoke the fire about every two hours during the night.

Would you like to try climbing out from under your warm covers in the middle of a freezing night to get more wood from the wood box? The floor at those times felt like a chunk of ice. By the time you could get socks and shoes on, your whole body was shivering and you were wide-awake.

If the fire being stoked was in the kitchen fireplace, that meant that the hallway between the kitchen portion of the house and the bedroom and living portion had to be crossed and the north wind blowing through that north south hallway had to be endured before you arrived at the kitchen wood box.

Believe me: by the time you were at the fire-building task, you were wide-awake.

It was expected that you would accomplish this task at 2:00 a.m. without waking the rest of the household.

Returning to the bed to disappear under the pile of quilts and blankets with your clothes on, having removed only your shoes, was the quickest way to regain some comfort and become convinced again that you were not going to freeze.

It was pure heaven, on the other hand, to arise, when called, at 6:00 a.m. only to find that an older brother had fired up the stove and two fireplaces and had the living room and kitchen toasty warm, a pan of forty golden brown biscuits setting on the back of the stove to keep them warm and awaiting the cooking of the eggs and bacon.

Not all the memories are of the discomforts and deprivations; some are of the grand rewards of enjoying some of the best cooked and choicest food on the planet.

By the time the fall season had arrived and settled in, in a rewarding way, about the first of October, most of the crops were harvested. Most of the vegetables and fruits had been picked, preserved, pickled, or canned in mason jars. Most of the potatoes had been bunked and dry beans and peas had been shelled, winnowed, dusted with pyrethrins contained in Bee Brand Insect Powder to control weevils, and stored in metal containers that were rodent proof.

Farm cats were allowed to come and go at will inside to the comfort of the fireplace in the winter, so mice and rats were mostly under control.

Adding freshly cooked cane syrup to the breakfast menu described above was always a delight, as the harvest of our cane and making of syrup began about October 15 and continued until finished.

Cane syrup was a universal barter item during the Great Depression just as were the eggs. It was just that more families produced eggs. The making of syrup required a greater investment in equipment and know-how than most families could afford.

By cane-grinding time, the winter vegetables were growing well, turnips, collards, cabbages, radishes, beets, onions, Irish potatoes, and carrots were staple winter-growing plants, and we grew them all. Strawberry plants were planted in the fall. We protected them from freezing by covering them with pine straw, which was readily available in the piney woods.

Such was the cycle of the season for ensuring a constant and abundant supply of nutritious food for the family, for sharing with neighbors who needed help, and for grown children to take with them when they departed for their new homes after visits to the homestead.

# CHAPTER 8
# Grass: Times Do Change

Our perspectives on many things change as time moves on, especially during the change from childhood to adulthood and especially if your childhood occurred during the Great Depression of the 1930s. Of all things that I view differently from how I viewed them as a child growing up on a subsistence farm in the piney woods in the 1930s, one of the most outstanding is grass.

I made a brief reference to this in my earlier book, *Collard Greens*. It deserves more attention.

To this eight-year-old in 1933, grass was a dirty word. No matter that the cows, horses, goats, mules, and pigs ate grass and relied on it for sustenance, and we in turn relied on them. My primary occupation when not at school was fighting grass. Grass was my hated, deadly enemy. It stole my playtime. It made my back hurt. It loomed as a lifetime threat to my well-being.

There was a special hoe that was of just the right weight, and just the right length of handle, to be ideal for use by a certain eight-year-old of limited strength. It was a gooseneck hoe compared to a heavier model hoe with an eyelet into which a handle was placed.

I never had to worry about the hoe being available for my use when the grass-killing assignment showed up on my after-school agenda. That was my hoe, as much as if I had bought it with my own money. Quite a consideration when I had never had enough money to purchase anything as expensive as a hoe. Yet the supreme need for a hoe to be available for use by this eight-year-old when his assignment called for him to hoe, scrape, and cut the grass and other weeds from around the eternal cotton, corn, peanuts, and sweet potatoes, plus all of the garden plants, and hill them up with a base of mulched topsoil to conserve moisture had somehow preempted the spending of the money on anything else in order to provide Ard with a hoe.

In addition to the grass that would be killed by that hoe, the character of that boy was being molded into the work ethic of the family. Every family member of the household had assigned tasks which were suited to his/her size, strength, and age or slightly above to develop more muscles and to inculcate in each one the habit of doing all the work possible, as that seemed to be the only way to survive.

We had frequent reminders of the supreme virtue of work by clichés: "If a man wants to eat, he has to be willing to work." "You earn your bread by the sweat of your brow." "If you expect to amount to anything in life, you have to be willing to work *from can to can't*."

It is important to realize that the boy, the nominal owner of the hoe, did not really own the hoe; it was a family possession which was set aside for killing grass and forming the character of one individual only, yours truly.

This formational arrangement continued in position all through my school years until I finished high school, not long before my seventeenth birthday.

It had its effect.

There was no place in my limited experience with Bermuda grass that led me to believe that Bermuda grass would ever have an economic use. No matter that the grass had been brought to the Sylvest farm for the noble purpose of feeding livestock in the form of hay. In that mode, the animals ate the grass, seeds and all. The seeds passed through the animal's digestive tract, none the worse for wear, so when deposited in the dung of the animal there was the viable seed germinating in the rich fertilizer of the manure and growing into the perpetual nuisance that I perceived Bermuda grass to be.

The origin of the grass on our farm was not necessarily that of being hauled there as hay. It required only one visiting horse which had eaten Bermuda grass hay for supper the night before at some hostel, barn, or stage stop twenty miles down the road to deposit enough seed in one pile to ensure the infestation of the family farm for the next forty years.

I quickly learned that killing Bermuda grass was to occupy my spare time for the foreseeable future. It remained so for the ensuing nine years, until 1942.

Not to be outdone by the important role played by Bermuda grass, there was the ever present threat that Johnson grass seed or seeds of cockleburs would float downstream in McKim's Creek from the farm of some neighbor farmer. So, each spring there was a campaign that began when vegetation began to grow on the Sylvest farm and other farms of the neighborhood. It consisted in getting all the members of the family not occupied in more royal legitimate pursuits to walk with the instruments of war upon grass—hoes, cane knives, shovels, and a burlap bag in which we gathered the invasive, strange grasses and weeds—for removal before they could live long enough to reproduce and deposit God's abundance in the form of nuisance grass or weed seed on our property.

This process was called "roguing." Roguing was identified as the recommended method of removing "rogue," or undesirable plants, otherwise officially called "weeds" in proper parlance of the Land Grant College agronomists. To them, the definition of a weed is "any plant that is out of place."

Believe you me: there were plenty of plants "out of place" on the Sylvest farm.

This tactic worked remarkably well for a number of years as we kept our fields and gardens free of Johnson grass and cockleburs until I graduated from high school.

This time of the 1930s predates the widespread use of chemicals to control weeds and insects.

Between Bermuda grass infestation and the boll weevil, the cotton industry would not have remained king long without chemical controls of both insects and weeds.

It seems an easy thing to envision not using chemicals to control these pests; however, without the use of chemicals, the amount of cotton that could be grown in the world would not nearly meet the needs of today's population.

The same applies to other crops for food and fiber as well as feed for livestock.

Bermuda grass was commonly called wiregrass by many in our community during the 1930s. I was not deceived. When either one was mentioned, I got the backache just thinking about my trustworthy hoe. I was an expert on chopping cotton and hoeing corn and garden crops to include peanuts, Irish potatoes, and sweet potatoes.

When I walk around the neighborhood in the twenty-first century and see the beautiful green lawns of St. Augustine, Centipede, and other hybrid derivative lawn grasses, well fertilized and with weeds controlled by application of selective herbicides, I am reminded of the time when I was certain that the only enemy of Bermuda grass in the whole world was me and my hoe.

Do not be misled by my apparent obsession with Bermuda grass; we hated and fought the other common grasses and all weeds in our fields and gardens with equal fervor: crab grass, Johnson grass, nut grass, Dallis grass, and on down the litany of noxious species and varieties.

No wonder my mind rebels whenever the mention of fertilizing grass comes up.

My old back remembers the time when that would have been unheard of and a mental image of that hoe comes along with the backache.

The necessity of using hoes to control grass around crops was such that sometimes whole gangs of hoe hands would be hired simultaneously to chop cotton and clean grass from the crop.

All of the required hoeing could not possibly be done by small children with their small tools. However, knowledgeable parents were wise enough to teach their children to work and do all portions of the job themselves, as that would save the cost of paying wages for hoe hands.

I recall that my brother, Frankie, had a field of cotton on the old Provencal homestead in which the grass and weeds were so bad as to be nearly out of control. Frank hired eight hoe hands. One of them was named Homer

Smith. Homer Smith was known to be the champion hoe hand of the entire surrounding countryside. He was so good with a hoe that a legend was told about him having been sent to the Louisiana State Penitentiary for some infraction, and it was during his time in prison that he developed his expertise with the hoe. I was unable to verify this story. However, Mr. Homer Smith was no doubt the champion hoe hand of the community. So, Frank paid Homer a premium of fifty cents per day extra to stay ahead of the gang. That meant not to let any member of the gang clean as many feet of grassy rows as he at any point during the day. Frank further challenged the other members of the gang with the incentive that any hoe hand that hoed more that Homer did would be paid an extra dollar for his day's work.

The challenges motivated the gang and a friendly competitive atmosphere seemed to contribute to the cheerful accomplishment of more work.

I was just glad I was not expected to hoe all that cotton myself. I felt very small and insignificant standing alone with my hoe in a five-acre field of cotton.

The hoe was not the only instrument of war against grass and weeds. Plows of several descriptions were designed for the task. All the plows we had were made to be pulled by mules or horses.

The most commonly used plow was known as the Georgia stock. It was made of a wooden beam about eight feet long. Two straps of iron about two inches wide, a quarter of an inch thick, and two feet long were bolted together in a configuration such that it could be bolted to the beam to form a foot. Metal plows, such as shovels, sweeps, and heel sweeps, and coulters, were fastened to the foot by means of a heel bolt. The bolt was about six inches long and three-quarters of an inch in diameter with a substantial washer and a wing nut made so that it could be tightened with a hammer to hold the selected plow points or adaptations on the foot of the plow.

Plow handles for the walking operator to use in controlling the plow were fastened to the rear of the beam.

This plow was usually outfitted with a shovel and a heel sweep, which when pulled by the mule would leave a furrow about six inches deep and eighteen inches wide. That was quite a swath of soil to move in one pass down the row in the field. A lot of grass was killed in this way.

Another local favorite was a spring-toothed harrow, again, made so one man controlled the plow as the mule pulled the plow down the length of the row. The operator had to keep the path of the mule and the location of the plow so that the small plow point on each spring plowed a furrow in the right spot along the row so the small grass growing there was uprooted, allowing the sun to dry out the roots and kill the grass. At least that was the purpose of the exercise. It worked amazingly well.

The day I graduated from high school at Provencal in Natchitoches Parish, I gathered up the nerve to ask my dad if I could leave immediately and enroll in Louisiana State University 175 miles away in Baton Rouge.

His answer was, "Son, I hate for you to leave me with all that grass in the corn."

I found my oldest sister, Dixie Moss, a schoolteacher, and told her what he had said. Her reply was, "You had better get off this hill while you can. There will always be grass to kill on this place."

It was never to be forgotten that the formation of the character of the child using the hoe, plow, or other implement or tool was also central to the purpose of the exercise.

Much like my experience in trying to market my skills in goat management, I never found a ready market for skills in killing grass with a hoe or with horse-drawn equipment.

As for the character development, I'll have to let you consult my siblings and other peers to get a read on how effective that effort by my parents turned out in my case.

I can vouch for one thing: the impression that grass was my eternal enemy was indelibly stamped on my brain forever.

# CHAPTER 9
# Royce Takes a Walk

Two-year-olds can provide endless challenges. Royce was a two-year-old in the fall of 1932. It was a mild autumn, and we had just finished our cane-grinding, syrup-making season.

Minnie, John D, Frank, Spurgeon, Pauline Ruth, and I were engaged in ongoing farmwork and chores. It was in the afternoon when we had finished with the noontime meal, which we called dinner, as opposed to the evening meal, which we called supper.

We had eaten and gone back to our varied tasks.

Typically, as these activities went on, Ruth, aged four, and Royce played around whatever family member they chose around the house and yard, an area of about half an acre. It had not been but a few months since Royce had given us all a scare by falling asleep and slept for over an hour under the dirty clothes pile in the middle of the day and no one knew where he was.

Suddenly, someone asked about Royce. Everyone looked around and at each other; no Royce was to be seen. Just two and a half years old, he couldn't have gone far. We all looked in the most frightening and dangerous places first, like the well, and around the lot where we kept all the animals. With every one of us on the run, we could cover a lot of ground in a few minutes.

We looked everywhere. No Royce. Frank, Spurgeon, and Papa began searching for tracks. Anyone walking, even a baby, would leave footprints in dust or mud, and all the hill folks knew how to track.

No signs of that two-year-old's footprints could anyone find. We fanned out in all directions.

Frank had headed across the field and down the wagon road toward the syrup mill then located on McKim's Creek, which flowed across John D's woods and fields. The mill was about a quarter mile from the house, a long ways for a two-year-old to walk.

Frank screamed, "He came this way! Here's his footprint!" We ran as fast as we could, because we knew where Royce was headed. He loved the mules, wagon, and syrup mill, and he was not old enough to know we had finished the grinding season so he was clearly headed for his favorite place, the syrup mill.

We all knew that the mill was on the other side of the creek. Royce would have to cross the creek to get to the mill.

Oh, my God! Please don't let my little brother drown crossing that creek. The creek was shallow enough for Royce to cross by wading if he didn't fall down and get swept away by the current into deeper water.

It was really a small stream for an adult to cross, but for a two-year-old?

Frank, who had outdistanced us all, yelled again, "Here he is! He's okay!"

What relief! That baby could have drowned as easily as he had waded safely across the creek, about six feet wide and six inches deep.

Royce had crossed that creek. He was standing up on the other bank in the middle of the wagon road, where he was looking at all of us and smiling. He was just where he wanted to be, almost to the syrup mill only two hundred feet away.

He just seemed to be enjoying all the attention. Every family member had to give him a hug. The adults took turns carrying Royce back to the house.

This made two times in his third year Royce had scared us all half to death, and he had done nothing a two-year-old should not be expected to do: fall asleep in the dirty clothes pile and take a long walk by himself to the syrup mill.

# CHAPTER 10
# The Mule versus the Tractor

As hard as it may seem to the reader of these pages, there were still legitimate claims as to the relative efficiency of mules versus tractors during the Great Depression. Most plowing that was done on the thousands of subsistence hill farms throughout the South was still done by horsepower in the 1920s and 1930s.

There must have been no more germane or more widely used subject for debate in Future Farmers of America high school parliamentary procedure classes across the states of the South than the debate over the tractor and the mule. I remember our agriculture teacher at Provencal High School in 1939, W. A. Koonzie, setting that proposition to two debating teams when I was a freshman in the eighth grade. The class was studying parliamentary procedure, and the rules for debate were being studied.

I do not remember who was on the teams or what the defenders of their positions declared during the debate. I do remember that the debate was real, and it left me pondering the proposition. At that time, I remember feeling uncertain whether I would ever be prosperous enough to own my own mule, let alone a tractor.

Moving to a higher platform for education in 1942, I found the argument still raging among the agricultural students living with me in the dormitory rooms of the Dairy Pavilion on the campus of Louisiana State University, where the student workers at the dairy and milk processing plant called the creamery lived.

Two who were susceptible to getting into this argument were Jack Stanley, of Leesville, Louisiana, and Erin Foster of Merryville, Louisiana. Foster invariably took the part of defending the valiant mule. Stanley always took the part of the tractor.

It would be important, in evaluating the evidence and arguments they advanced, to know enough about the attributes each defender attached to his favorite. Both very bright students, this debate could go on for hours without either yielding a major point to his opponent.

Foster relied heavily on his experience of growing up on his father's farm, which was powered by mules. Stanley, whose father was a high school principal, might have been a bit more familiar with the cash income from a teacher's salary available to purchase fuel for a tractor than Foster. Foster made the point that the farmer with mules grew his own fuel in the form of corn. Stanley would retort that mules ate twelve months of the year and the cost of that feed could be saved as a tractor only consumed fuel when it was running.

Actually, this author, an agricultural economics major, was to learn later in class and in life that Foster and Stanley both had valid arguments and the circumstances often could be the determining factor in what the best business decision was.

The arguments often relied upon by the defenders of mule power espoused much about what economists refer to as managing by the least cost combination. You could see that, given the right circumstances, it would be less costly to have mules that, if on the right farm, with excellent pasture, could virtually feed themselves and not require much cost to maintain and perform work. Certainly a valid argument. The mule side of the debate usually carried glowing descriptions of how the mules could be used as saddle mounts, which was highly valuable in the woods around Provencal where cattle, hogs, and goats had to be herded and protected until sold for market. A tractor could not meet that need very well.

However, the converse argument was that the tractor was going to become the vehicle by which more work could be done per man-hour than with a mule. This argument leans away from operating on a least-cost basis to another economic principle: the purpose of being in business is to maximize profits, not to minimize costs.

So the argument would go on and on.

I only wish I could recall the actual arguments of those two students. Jack Stanley went on to get his doctorate and became the head of the agriculture department at Nicholls State University. Orin Foster worked briefly for the LSU Agricultural Extension Service, I believe, and left to establish what became a successful insurance business in Natchitoches Parish.

It was years before the mule-admiration society almost totally disappeared from the American scene. A good working pair of mules faithfully following the commands of the mule skinner is still a thing of beauty. Not much money in it, but a sight to admire.

Least cost combination indeed.

My preparatory exposure to qualify me for participating in the mule-tractor argument was real and lengthy. I followed John D, Vince, Frankie, and Spurgeon on every occasion I could get permission when they were using mules to work or ride.

Before I learned to walk, Vince would take me from my mother's bed early in the morning, put me on his back, and head for the pastures and barns to round up the cows and mules.

Nothing ever entertained me more than watching our mules, Jane and Pearl, jump over a three-foot fence at the poles when Vince removed the top two poles to lower the height. Poles were often used for this purpose on the piney woods farms, as no actual steel hinges, extremely scarce items, were required, as was the case with gates.

One time, Ernest Bell, a logger, our school bus driver, and dear friend, was hauling logs off our farm. A mule owner named Jimmie Jones had four mules he used to bunch and load the logs.

As sometimes happened in logging, in the hills of the piney woods of North Louisiana, the truck became stuck in the mud. After the usual struggle of rocking back and forth, Mr. Bell called for the team. Before long, this ten-year-old was fully entertained by Jimmie Jones hooking his team of four mules to that log truck loaded with logs to pull it out of the mud hole.

Now, it is important to this story that you know something about the four mules. Three of the mules were Missouri mules. That is, they were dark in color and had whitish-gray noses. All three of them were the same size.

The fourth mule was red. From listening to the Jimmie Jones/John D Sylvest conversation earlier, a risky business itself for a ten-year-old (adult business in which children are to be seen but not heard), I had learned that the red mule was a young mule which Mr. Jones was training to be a log mule.

That was the reason that the red mule was one of the lead mules, the two in front. Reliable, experienced mules of the foursome would naturally be placed as the "wheel" pair.

Additionally, as the mule skinner (much more romantic term than "driver" to yours truly) walks to the rear on the right side of the team. That leaves his right arm free to handle his ever present whip if needed. Which mule was likely to need the most discipline? Of course, the young red mule, as he was still a student, if you can apply that term to a mule.

So, the red mule occupied the right front, or "off," position in the four-up team. For your edification, the opposite side was known as the "near" side.

I didn't know it at that moment but was to learn in a few minutes that I dearly had the ambition to grow up to become a mule skinner because I had seen Jimmie Jones do something I didn't know a living man could do. Yes, siree! I would become a mule skinner just like Mr. Jimmie Jones!

Jones hooked that foursome of mules to the front axle of that loaded log truck. I stood about thirty feet away and watched. Ernest Bell yelled, "Ready!" and raced the V-8 engine of the Ford log truck.

Jimmie Jones yelled, "Git up, Red!"

Four mules swung into action, planting their hooves in the moist soil and pulling with every muscle in their bodies, bellies nearly touching the ground as they stepped.

The truck rocked to an upslope position in the mud hole and Jones hollered, "Hold, Red!" But the young mule did not get the message. Red released the pressure he had on his collar and stood back and relaxed. When the red mule did that, the truck rolled back down the slope and pulled the other three mules of the team with it.

Did that stop Jones? No, sir!

Out came that fifteen-foot bullwhip swinging over Jones's head. "I said, 'Hold, Red!'"

*Wham! Pow!*

Around came that whip, slamming into Red's broadside.

*Kerplop!* You could have heard that sound one hundred yards away as 1,200 pounds of red mule hit the dirt. That red mule dropped to the ground, broadside, like a huge sack of sand.

No living man can knock a 1,200-pound mule down with a bullwhip with one lick.

Jimmie Jones did!

Dropped one red mule to the ground, four legs sticking out and shivering in every muscle.

Jones yelled, "Git up, Red!"

As Bell powered the engine, the team moved, and the truck inched forward until the stuck wheel was again up on the slope. Jones again yelled, "Hold, Red!"

That mule and the other three held the tense maximum pressure on their collars until Bell and his helper had put limbs and logs under the dual wheels, supporting them perfectly for Bell to drive out of the mud.

Jones said, "Whoa!" When the mules stopped, he unhooked them and drove them to the side.

As he did, Jones walked up to the red mule and patted him on the shoulder, saying, "That's the way, Red. Good mule. Good mule."

Yes, sir! Right then and there, I decided I was going to grow up to be a mule skinner like Mr. Jimmie Jones! Who would want an old hunk of metal called a tractor when he could have mules instead. Mules have names and personalities.

Besides, if you can't find cash with which to buy gasoline, how are you going to keep a tractor running?

A depression might not always be regarded as a bad thing if you look at all the opportunities it provided to learn lessons of lifelong importance on subjects, such as, "Which is best: mules or tractors?"

# CHAPTER 11
# Fence Building

When the decision had been made to clear land and grow crops of any kind other than timber in the piney woods of the South, it meant that the decision maker had decided to fence in the area to be farmed. The reason for this is the laws of the time allowed owners of farm animals to permit the animals to range freely over all unfenced land.

Before the Europeans arrived in this country, the Indians used very little fencing. They guarded the areas where they grew their crops. Great jobs for children of the civilization which did not have organized schools.

When Europeans introduced a more intensive cultivation of crops and husbandry of animals, they brought with them the knowledge, skills, and habits of their original country for fencing in fields and pastures.

In the stony ground of New England, the normal fences were often made of the stones which had to be removed from the fields before they were planted. Actually, the availability of the stones of usable size often determined how large and in what shape the field would be arranged. Digging postholes in a ground filled with large stones in many cases was very difficult, if not impossible.

When the topography was hills, valleys, and flowing streams, the shapes of the fields were often dictated by the location of the most level land. It is hard to plow on a hillside. That is one obstacle that faced settlers of the hilly and mountainous areas of the South.

The Sylvest homestead was typical of this. McKim's Creek traversed the 160-acre farm, in the shape of a square one-half mile on each side. McKim's ran from the northwest corner to the southeast corner. The most level land was along the floodplains of the creek. Other land level enough to clear it of trees and plant row crops was near the top of hills where slopes were mostly gentle.

Building fences around the cleared land was done on the Sylvest farm using the same plans and skills that had been used from the beginning of the settling of the country. The principle applied was to make use of the materials and tools that you have available. This often translated into cutting the timber and splitting the logs into lengths and shapes that made it usable for worm-rail fences, or what we called "pew" fences.

The worm-rail fence was typically built by splitting rails from the downed timber from clearing. The standard length of the rails was nine feet. This length was pretty well determined by the fact that when cutting logs it was much harder to find a log that would make good rails, split straight if cut into lengths longer than nine feet. Also, slender rails longer than nine feet would bend, so their effectiveness against pressure, including animals trying to break through, was not as good.

This splitting process was not for people of weak back or character. It was hard work.

First, select the log to be split. Position it in such a manner that it could withstand the blow of a sledgehammer or steel wedge driven by a wooden maul without rolling over.

This sometimes required placing a rail or two rails already split against the log to hold it still. The splitting process was then begun by placing a steel wedge against the end of the log and striking the steel wedge with a light blow from a sledgehammer, thus marking the end of the log with a line denominating the diameter of the circular end of the log. After this was done, the wedge was then driven into the end of the log, care being taken to getting the splitting process started without missing the line previously drawn. If necessary, two or three steel wedges were used to assure the success of this step. Only a few of the original strokes for driving the steel wedges into the wood were made with the steel sledgehammer, as more would "strawberry" the wedge or cause the edges to curl up and make the wedge no longer useful. So, after the wedge was firmly stuck into the log, a wooden maul was used. The maul was made by selecting a tough variety of tree nearby, such as hickory, oak, sweet gum, or black gum. Care was given to finding a specimen that was straight enough and of about the right diameter, about six inched in diameter, and with a limb free area about five feet long. Typically, a five-foot length was cut from the tree. The smaller end of the log was carved with an axe until it formed a handle about three feet long. The remaining of the five-foot log became the six-inch diameter, two-foot-long "hammer" section of the maul. This green wood, roughly hewn tool was very effective in driving steel wedges into the logs being split for rails and pews for fence building.

Two men with a crosscut saw, axes, wedges, and mauls could split about two ten-inch pin oak logs in a half day into from ten to twenty fence rails or pews. That would be enough to construct about twenty to forty feet of fence, depending upon the type of fence being constructed.

When the initial split opened a half-inch crack, the splitting process could be continued by striking the log in the crack with an axe, carefully aiming at splinters of wood that tended to hold the halves of the log together. As these splinters were cut with the axe, the crack in the log gradually opened wider and it became easier to cut the remaining splinters with the axe.

After the log was split in half, the process was repeated for each half of the log. Sometimes the halves were split into two rails, and other times they were split into three or four, depending upon the size of the log.

Frequent sharpening of tools was rewarded by the sharper blades, which made the job easier and faster. So much time was spent sharpening tools that much of it was done after dark when splitting could not be done. Often I saw my father and brothers sharpening tools by the fireside in our living room after the chores were done and it was nearing bedtime. Other times I saw one of them in the blacksmith shop hammering steel wedges into their original shape for use the next day.

I learned as I watched.

Much of the sharpening was done in the blacksmith shop on the farm where it could be done not only by forging but by the manually operated grinding wheel against which the tool could be held while the person pumped the lever, turning the wheel with one or both feet depending upon the design of the grinder. Heavier forging work, such as making new wedges, was usually done at factories, of which there were few to none in the state.

Of course, filing could be done either in the shop, by the fireside, or in the woods. Files were usually carried in our pockets.

Not every year, but from time to time, new wedges and axes had to be purchased. Steel wedges were not driven into the logs with the steel sledgehammer, for that would have caused the head of the wedges to flatten and strawberry out so they would have to be ground down and dissipated too quickly. Instead, we cut wooden mauls from tough timber, such as young hickory. The trunk of eight inches in diameter was cut into four-foot lengths, and the timber was placed in the top of the blacksmith shop to cure. When a new maul was needed, this work could be done at night. A four—or five-foot log was selected, and axe reduction of about thirty-four inches of the forty-eight—to sixty-inch piece of timber was done. The rough handle that resulted was trimmed further with a drawknife until a respectable handle resulted. Then the handle was smoothed by taking a piece of broken window glass and scraping it until the handle was as smooth as the handle of a new claw hammer or hatchet.

In this hand manufacturing process, several tools were used almost interchangeably. One might change from an axe to a hatchet because his arm was getting tired. Or, in order to be able to sit and yet continue the process, the drawknife might be the tool of choice. Sometimes there would arise a situation in the trimming, cleaning, and dressing of the handle that would just make the use of the old faithful pocketknife the tool of choice.

I have seen respectable duck decoys carved with the only tool used being the pocketknife.

With these sharp, cutting instruments, the further splitting of the log, which we had just left in halves in our above description, could proceed with amazing speed. An oak log nine feet long, twelve inches in diameter at the "butt" end, and eight inches in diameter at the top end would usually split into four to six rails. Larger logs could make more rails, but if the logs were too large, the time required to split out each rail was greater so smaller logs were preferred. Several varieties of oak and pine were the favored trees for making rails as they split more readily than other trees.

We never tried to split gum trees, as they required too much work. Knotty trees (i.e., those with many large limbs) were culled out with the gum trees. Crooked trees were rejected as well.

The rails resulting from this hand harvesting and manufacturing process were ready to use when split. They were laid in a zigzag line with corners describing about a sixty-degree angle. One row was added upon another until the fence was about nine rails high. This was high enough to discourage a grown cow from attempting to jump over or push aside such a fence. When placing the rails in position, if the end of a rail was too large, sometimes we would cut a notch in the thick end so the resulting crack from putting another rail on top of it would not be so wide that it tempted a pig, goat, or other farm animal to try to crawl through the crack.

By laying the rails so that one rail was laid with the butt end in one direction and the next rail put into that panel was placed in the opposite direction, the fence height could be managed so the fence was most level and stable at the end of construction.

I remember John D would come along and have the fencing crew replace a rail or trim another in order to get the finished quality of fence he desired. Such was the training process of growing up on a farm with many crops and animal enterprises. In later years, I chose to answer the question, "Where did you learn how to do that, boy?" with "On the farm by osmosis."

Growing up in this environment taught you so many things that it appeared to others with different experiences that you must have had to study hard to learn so much. Not so. Just osmosis.

One advantage of the worm-rail fence was that it did not require digging postholes, as there were no posts used in constructing it. It could be modified in construction to alternate rails of different lengths to get a bit more fence with less wood. One design used rails of nine feet in length alternating with rails of four feet in length. Another design used rails of nine feet in length alternated with rails of two feet in length. This design is so unstable and so likely to get knocked over that it was often reinforced by placing posts in the corners. Sometimes weights, such as logs or heavy rejected rails, were placed on top to stabilize the fence.

As you can see, there could be so many combinations of wood to form a fence that we could not describe them all.

One other design was used on the Sylvest homestead: the pew fence.

In the pew fence, the pews are split as in splitting rails except larger logs are used and the rails are slit into ever thinner segments until they resemble sawed boards. This makes them more suitable for nailing to posts than the heavier timbered rails. Posts are then placed at eight feet intervals and the pews are nailed to the posts. This kind of wooden fence lends itself to stopping the intrusion of hogs.

The wood can be nailed close together at the bottom of the fence and above about three feet two; three or more strands of barbed wire can be affixed to complete the barrier. The fence is thus rendered a good stop for all range farm animals.

The pews used in this type fence were turned into a position such that the thick or bark side of the pew was down when nailed to the fence. This turned the sides of the pew into a kind of gabled end and made the rainwater drain off the pew, drying it quicker after a rain so the wood would not rot as soon.

For those with the wherewithal, in which category we seldom seemed to fall, hog wire, which was woven wire from thirty-two inches upward, and came in rolls, could be nailed to posts and barbed wire added on top of it.

Some of our replacement fences in later years were made of hog wire topped with barbed wire.

On the surface, you can observe that land clearing and expansion of our crop and pasture acreages and partitioning off different sections for special purposes was continuous. There was always more to be done when higher priority jobs were not demanding our time and energy.

The old farm site, recently visited, would have to be cleared again if it were used for crops and pasture as it is covered with heavy timber, both pine and hardwood.

Like goat management, clearing land with hand tools I found not to be a highly marketable skill during my lifetime in the twentieth and twenty-first centuries in the USA.

# CHAPTER 12
# From Can to Can't

It was just recently that I spoke to someone and mentioned that when I was growing up, we worked "from can to can't."

Whereupon, a discussion arose as to what that means.

In our subsistence farming mode during the Great Depression of the 1930s, the rule of the household was that everyone who was not too ill, too young, or too old worked from as early in the morning as one could see how with no electricity, until it was so dark at the end of the day that one could not see how to work outdoors anymore. Many times, I milked cows and fed hogs, cows, and horses after dark and opened gates so the subject animals could access certain portions of pasture over night.

Our source of artificial light came from burning kerosene only in the summer months when the days were naturally longer plus the wood fire in the fireplace during the winter.

Often certain work could easily be done by moonlight and no artificial light was employed. However, nearly every household had several kerosene lamps and one or more kerosene lanterns, the former being designed for indoor use primarily and the latter for outdoor use.

Of course, anyone who has lived all his/her life with electricity would not appreciate the necessity of that and should not be expected to even pick up on the meaning of the phrase "from can to can't," a fact that had temporarily escaped me.

Not only was the phrase used to describe our daily routine, it was used to describe the same rule throughout the entire community. There was no one, but no one, in the piney woods where I grew up who would not agree to live by, and fully understand what working "from can to can't," meant. It flat meant scratching for a living with every means available, which included taking advantage of every minute of daylight to grow and preserve food and procure the basic necessities of life.

In order to grasp the general sense of this attitude, it is essential that one realize that the difficulty of life on that sand hill without electricity or powered implements was little different from the way poor people lived five hundred years earlier.

It was more difficult than some of the population living five hundred years earlier, many of whose major manufacturing operations were run by waterpower or windmills. Not so for many of us in the hills of the piney woods of the South during the Great Depression.

True, steam power, internal combustion power, and waterpower had all been invented, but that did not mean that any one was available to the typical homesteader. That is the reason we shelled the corn each week by hand and took enough to the local McGaskey gristmill on Saturdays to provide corn meal to last a week.

Getting access to that gristmill, which was powered by an old automobile engine, was essential. Services of this kind were sought out wherever they were available in the community, and most of them were accessed by horse—or mule-drawn wagon, buggy, or horseback for the typical family. The typical family did not own a gasoline-powered gristmill or a motorized means of transportation.

About half of the families did not own a wagon or cart with which to haul anything. They had to borrow or otherwise work out an arrangement with a neighbor who did own a wagon to haul anything they needed moved. The typical arrangement worked like this. I will come help you cut and harvest your sugarcane to make syrup if you will haul my cane to the syrup mill. Thus a barter arrangement was worked out so labor was traded for the use of a team and wagon or for syrup or other produce.

Sometimes, as with the grinding of corn at the gristmill, the barter was just a matter of taking a toll of the product involved.

The routine of "from can to can't" is defined by the rising of the sun. As soon as enough light was provided by the dawning sun to see how to feed animals, sharpen tools, prepare food, and otherwise begin the activities of the day, those activities were begun each morning.

This meant that, as fire obtained by burning wood could be done when a match was struck, it did not have to be daylight. That particular chore was carried on before sunrise. That saved precious daylight hours to be used in doing those other activities which cannot be done during the hours of darkness, such as chopping Bermuda grass from around cotton plants or corn stalks.

While the "from can to can't" implementation seems to require a lot of organization, all that formula had been worked out already as the years went by and habit had taken over. Every subsistence farmer had the same routine, and all family members conformed to it. For example, you can feed animals before daylight, as they can see well enough to consume their hay or grain. However, you could not see well enough in the darkness to plow the crops, as you might plow them up and destroy them.

A rather parallel expression to "from can to can't" was that of "getting up and going to bed with the chickens." This expression did not mean that we had chickens in our beds. It just meant that the time of day that chickens descend from their roosting spot and begin their activity for the day occurs precisely according to the sun's rising. When enough light is provided by the sun, the chickens come off the roost and begin to forage.

When it got so dark with the setting of the sun that chickens could no longer see to search for food, they climbed on to their roost and went to sleep. Hence, the expression "going to bed and getting up with the chickens" grew to merely mean going to bed early and getting up early. Sometimes it meant that your daily schedule of activity was controlled by the light provided by the sun and not artificially by electricity. Like chickens do, you arise and go to work at daylight and quit work and go to bed at dark.

From "can to can't" simply means from daylight until dark, the same daily schedule as that followed by chickens. It means from the time you can see until the time that you can't see.

# CHAPTER 13
# Clearing Land

When John D and Minnie Fendlason Sylvest arrived at the 160-acre piney woods homestead below Provencal, Louisiana, in 1923 the place had only about twelve acres of cleared land.

This did not intimidate the new owners who were familiar with clearing land, having assisted in that activity from their childhood in the Washington Parish piney woods since before the turn of the century.

This brazen pair had eloped to get married on June 28, 1905, in Washington Parish.

John D was at home in Washington Parish working on his father's farm. After their marriage, they purchased a small plot of land on Sylvest Road about six miles below Franklinton near John D's parents, Nehemiah and Lenora Jane Sylvest. There they built their first home, a log cabin. Soon thereafter, they, with other members of their family and some neighbors, became charter members of Bethel Baptist Church, which has an active congregation over a hundred years later. Indeed, both of my parents are buried there.

In the same community as the church, they joined in the organization efforts of the first school in that part of Washington Parish.

My siblings, Dixie Edna, born June 28, 1906, and Artie Ora, born February 4, 1908, became two of the first students to attend that school. Vince Edward, born December 4, 1909, was followed by Johnnie Chloe born, July 19, 1911, Frank Emanuel, born October 11, 1913, James Spurgeon, born July 23, 1914, were born in Washington Parish.

By the time Spurgeon was a baby, Dixie was eight years old and her parents were set on getting a Baptist education for their offspring. John D and Minnie picked up their growing family and moved them to Pineville, where Louisiana College was being organized. They bought a home near the site of the new educational institution and John D was employed in much of the building process at the college, having contracted the job of installing all of the windows in the new three-story administration building.

A settlement developed around the new college and John D earned his living as a carpenter and a contractor there for a time. At some point in time, he opened a restaurant. Vince told me of his job of using a mule and a slide to haul the leftovers from the restaurant to the hogs which John D was raising in a pen, at the time, the modern way of acquiring pork and lard required to feed a large family.

(Not yet having arrived on the scene, the author had to rely on what he was told by his older siblings and parents about this time period.)

This family lived in Pineville, Louisiana, until 1923.

Pauline, who had been born in Pineville July 16, 1919, was the youngest living child when the family moved to Provencal on March 1, 1923.

From 1923 until 1938, John D and his sons continued to clear land in the pioneer fashion at Provencal.

Hand tools with a team of mules for power were all the resources available.

The primary tool was an axe. A double-bit axe with a head weighing four and a half pounds was John D's favorite tool. An average sized man of five feet, nine inches height and weight of about 160 pounds, it amazed me that he could do so much work that required so much strength. He could swing that ax with purpose and expected his sons to learn to do the same. We did.

The first step in clearing land was to select and define the area which was to be cleared. This being piney woods with hills, topography was an important factor. Drainage had to be considered. Only well-drained soil could be expected to be productive of row crops, one of our primary agronomic endeavors. Further, land that sloped too steeply would be subject to erosion from runoff water. If drainage was not naturally present due to the contours of the land and the soil was waterlogged, it was not the best cropland.

Cursory inspection usually sufficed to identify the acres set aside for clearing.

About 1926, which precedes my memory, John D set aside nine acres of woodland located in the creek bottom of the farm and across the McKim's Creek from the house. This was a fine way to occupy the time of boys like Vince, Frankie, and Spurgeon, who were all in their teens. From about 1932 on, my memory is most keen about the clearing process because I began to be involved in it personally by carrying jugs of drinking water and lunch to the work crew and running other errands.

As with all boys, those menial tasks to this kid were not rewarding. I wanted to be involved in the "grown-up" work of the men. However, that was to come, in time, for I had neither the muscles nor the strength at age seven to wield a four and one-half pound double-bit axe or to pull one end of a crosscut saw made for two grown men to use in cutting trees.

The crew always carried the crosscut saw, at least two axes, one grubbing hoe, a tool called a tie maul with a hammer face on one side and a wedge like face on the other. It was typically hammered with a wooden mallet which was made in the farm shop. Some steel wedges and some carved wooden wedges called gluts were additional commonplace tools. A member of the saw crew usually carried a soft drink bottle of kerosene, which we called coal oil, as the original product probably came from coal rather than the modern petroleum fraction. The top of the bottle was stopped by a branch of pine straw off a pine tree which provided a perfect device for dispensing just a bit of lubrication to the crosscut saw when it was being used to cut pine trees that were filled with sticky turpentine. We just filled the bottle about three-fourths full of kerosene, broke off one head of a pine branch, held the needles tightly together, and chopped them off about three inches above the top of the bottle with an axe.

I can see the sawyer, usually one of my older brothers, with the saw beginning to bind because of the accumulation of turpentine on the blade, reach for the bottle of kerosene carried in his right hip pants pocket, swing the bottle upside down, pointing at the saw blade and dripping just enough lubrication on the saw blade to make the turpentine release and free the blade for more cutting. While this act was in process, the blade of the saw was held so that the flat side of the blade was exposed. All of this action took only a few seconds. Then the saw blade was turned over and the exercise was repeated.

This was the process used when cutting the pine trees. Many of the trees were hardwood. There were lots of oak, hickory, sweet gum, elm, and ash, to name a few.

When the kerosene ran out, or was not handy for some reason, the resin from the pine tree could be cleaned from the saw blade by cutting hardwood trees instead for a while, then returning to complete the sawing of the pine.

There were little tricks of the trade like this which were learned from our elders and passed on from generation to generation.

It is amazing how proficient one can become in executing seemingly complicated and difficult tasks when given the opportunity to practice them daily. This opportunity seemed to be endless when work was being done by hand during the Great Depression.

The first step in clearing land after the area limits were defined was to ring the large trees which would be allowed to die from the ringing, making them easier to cut and remove and begin the process of the roots rotting in the ground for removal in future years. Ringing a tree consisted of chopping a groove about two inches deep all the way around the circumference of the tree.

Believe me: clearing land was no overnight activity. It took years to clear a new field of trees and underbrush by hand. The underbrush was removed first to give access to the larger trees to be cut. The resulting limbs and trash were piled against the standing trees and burned to hasten the process of killing the trees and removing them.

We called these piles of brush and limbs brush heaps. When a heap of brush was ready to burn, a younger member of the work crew, usually me it seemed, when I was large enough, would gather some fat lighter, the heart of mature pine trees which was heavily impregnated with the natural turpentine and tar ingredients of mature pines. This kindling served the purpose of starting a fire with highly flammable material to get the brush heap to burning rapidly.

Once well lit, the heap could be kept burning by rearranging the burning brush and limbs to manage the fire.

By age ten, I was considered just the right age for those activities.

When a large tree was cut, as most of them were, it came crashing to the ground, making a huge noise that could be heard for half a mile. In most cases, the trees were cut in such a manner that they would fall in a specific direction. By the time a boy could pull one end of a two-man crosscut saw, he was expected to know how to "bed" a tree and "throw" it. That is translated to cut a notch in the tree by sawing about 10 percent of the diameter of the tree in depth. Then cut with an axe chip from just above the saw cut to leave an opening toward which the tree would be inclined to fall, other factors being equal, such as lean of the tree and strength and direction of the wind. Throwing the tree simply meant making the tree fall in whatever direction the cutter chose.

This was accomplished by the proper bedding of the tree, compensating for the wind speed and direction, and when the saw had cut nearly through the tree the driving of the glut into the saw teeth track causing the tree to lean in the desired direction and topple just where you wanted it to go.

The gluts were usually made of dogwood and were cut out of a small dogwood tree about six inches in diameter. The wood, cut into blocks about twelve inches long, was placed in the overhead section of the farm blacksmith shop where the blocks could season, dry out, and shrink for six months or more. Actually, some such wood was kept there for this purpose on an ongoing basis. A slice of wood was split off the dogwood block with an ax. Then slabs of the wood were trimmed further with an ax or hatchet until they were roughly in the shape of a thinly tapered wedge, about twelve inches in length and about three inches wide. Then finer trim work was done with a pocketknife.

Every grown male in the region carried a good pocketknife, a tool essential to the repairing of harness and hundreds of other tasks that were performed daily.

It is strange to me that a pocketknife seems to be thought of these days only as a weapon. A farmer in the piney woods of the South would have been severely handicapped if he did not have ready access to a cutting blade like a pocketknife in his pocket. His knife was a tool as essential to his livelihood as was his axe.

One of the saw hands, called a sawyer, would carry a couple of the gluts in his pocket all day long or as long as he and his partner were felling trees.

An amazing thing about this operation was the relatively small amount of time it took to fell enough trees to keep the whole family busy for months assembling and burning the trunks, limbs, twigs, and leaves.

It took much longer with the crosscut saw to cut the down trees into lengths short enough for handling, in the form of rolling, lifting, and transporting them into piles called "log heaps."

The stumps of the largest trees presented the greatest problem. Sometimes parts of them they would remain in the ground for years before the land was totally cleared of stumps and roots.

I remember one winter when the Sylvest farm gave what was called a log rolling.

That meant that several families nearby were invited to join in a community effort to help move some logs in the Sylvest new ground that were too heavy and numerous for the family to move alone. Each family was asked to bring a cooked item, potluck style, so there would be plenty of food without overburdening the hostess with cooking duties.

At these functions, often the women and children went to the field where the work was being done and helped to pick up the trash, twigs, and limbs. The men would use their mule teams with chains to hook on to logs with tongs or grabs to drag the logs into good position in log heaps for burning.

This was extremely exciting for a young boy because he had a chance to observe the men he admired—his father, older brothers, and even neighbors he knew—participate in what appeared to be a big game as the entire work crew labored all day with teasing about whose mules could move the largest log, who could lift the most and pull the other down, etc.

The ladies had their role, and I often observed Ruth, my sister two years younger than I, helping my mother with food preparation, washing clothes, and doing many of the same land-clearing tasks I was doing when our mother was present.

Hand sticks were used along with cant hooks. The cant hooks were used to turn the logs when needed, such as positioning them to place grabs on them for snaking. Sometimes hand sticks were used to lift the smaller logs, which were not as heavy, and move them by hand. The hand stick was a stick usually made of seasoned hickory. It was about seven feet in length and about two and one-half inches in diameter, oval or somewhat square in shape, as they were typically handmade with an axe, adz, and drawknife. A hand stick can be placed on the ground with one end near the center of the log allowing for about 60 percent of the weight to be on one end of the log and 40 percent on the other. Then the log is rolled on to the hand stick so that two or three feet of the stick protrude from each side of the log. When the lifting crew of three is ready, the two men grab the hand stick, one on each side of the log, while the third member of the crew positions himself at the heaviest end of the log. All three men in the crew lift simultaneously on signal. The crew leader gives the signal. Three men can move a heavy load in this manner. When a log is lifted with a hand stick, the third crewmember, who is carrying the heavy end of the log, follows the other crewmembers to the destination. Coordination of effort is essential, as when either crewmember suddenly drops his load, unannounced, the other crewmembers are at severe risk of being injured. The log must be lifted gently, carried slowly, and let down gently. A good working crew of three men with hand sticks can move a lot of logs in a short time. It is tricky to get the hand stick under the log in the first step; typically, a cant hook is used. The weight of the log is expected to cause the hand stick to bend slightly in the middle so the log tends to remain in the middle between the hand stick partners, thus preventing the members of the team from being at risk that the log will roll in either direction and cause a problem.

Snaking the logs merely meant dragging them with the team of mules to the spot where they could be piled and burned. Since the log had to be dragged around stumps, standing trees, and other log heaps, it resulted in a crooked route, hence the coining of the phrase "snaking the logs."

A word about grabs. This is the logging industry name for a tool made of two pieces of iron about one inch wide and half an inch thick with a two—to four-inch long, spike shaped in one end of each like a hook. The opposite end of each of these two is attached to a ring placed through a hole near the end. The two welded rings are then connected to another large, heavy-duty ring into which a hook may be placed. These two pieces of iron, when driven into the opposite sides of a large log, provide the attachment by which a team of mules, horses, or oxen, or a tractor, can be connected to tow the log. Obviously, there are as many sizes of grabs as there are logs. A towing chain hook could simply be hooked into the common ring. A pair of grabs was about twenty-four inches long when picked up by the ring and weighed about five pounds. I distinctly remember that they could be carried by a boy ten years old or older.

Another device, of which John D had a good one, was a set of towing tongs. This device acted like the two irons of the grabs with the spikes on them. Two irons of which the tongs are made are attached to each other so that they have a scissors effect, causing the spikes to grip the log even tighter as the load is towed. Sometimes it was hard to get the spikes of these tongs out of the log after the pull was completed.

In the Sylvest field, the steam whistle which was blown at noon each day at the Weaver Lumber Company Mill at Flora, Louisiana, about five miles away, could be heard. Upon hearing this blast, which sounded much like the sound of a locomotive whistle, the workers would finish the job they were on and then move over to the wagon which was set up by the ladies with the food they had brought for the occasion. What a feast this was. Each lady had her favorite dishes and tried to outdo herself and everyone else by preparing the best dish possible. Plates were filled and diners found the most comfortable spots they could to eat. Some sat on the tongue of the wagon. Some found a handy stump nearby. Others say on a nearby log, and some just squatted where they were.

Shortly all were fed, and cold spring water, which I had brought from the nearest spring, was the drink for washing the food down.

One lady had taken the responsibility of making a big pot of coffee by putting grounds into a sack of muslin and boiling them in a pot over some coals from the many fires.

About 4 p.m., before the sun had set, each family headed home as each had the chickens to feed, cows to milk, and animals to be secured for the night before their long day would end long after dark.

The neighborly thing had been done. Fires would blaze from the log heaps and brush heaps. These fires had to be tended every few hours. Some of them would blaze for a week. This made an interesting sight when approaching the plot of new ground in the dark of night as flickering flames could be seen for miles.

Tending the fires was done to keep the burning pieces of logs close enough together to keep them burning. As the logs burned, they had a tendency to stop burning before they were completely consumed by fire. If kept close to other burning logs, the heat from each log radiated into the other, enabling the fire to continue burning until the two or three logs in the heap were burned up, totally consumed by the fire.

Good job for a boy, tending fires in the new ground. Gather all the limbs and brush from the ongoing clearing operation and keep piling them on the logs until all that was left was a pile of ashes.

## Cultivating Newly Cleared Land

When most of the trees had been cut and all loose residue had been burned, there was still much work to be done before new ground would be fully useful for cultivation.

Frankie and Spurgeon spent many hours grubbing out roots of trees and vines which did not disappear merely because the above ground portions of those plants had been cut off and burned. This was during the years I could remember, from about 1931 in my first year of school.

The grubbing hoe was a useful tool to determine if there was a root in the ground. It had the cutting edge of a heavy duty hoe only about three inches wide on one side and a cutting edge intended for cutting roots on the other. An oval handle about four feet in length made it a formidable tool.

There were invariably a few spots which seemed to be much freer of stumps and roots than the rest. Not to miss out on a single part of a crop, John D and Minnie knew from experience that new ground was richer than the old and some fine-tasting turnips could be coaxed to grow between the stumps and tree roots. A bull tongue shovel on the foot of a Georgia stock was just the plow to test the ground, stir the soil, and get some turnip and mustard seed into the ground. This was done in October.

Plowing under those conditions was almost impossible. By the time the plow stuck into the ground, the shovel struck a rook and jerked the mule and the plow hand sharply, sometimes resulting in bruised hands and legs from a whipping plow stock. I remember hitting a root, once, with the plow I was using. When the plow shovel caught on the root, the handles on the plow slammed into my side near my spleen and knocked the breath out of me. I hit the ground and groveled in pain.

Two thoughts were racing through my mind. One thought was concern for whether I was seriously injured. Another thought pressing to the surface of my consciousness was, "How am I going to stop that mule?" The mule was trained to keep walking and pulling until told to stop by voice command of "Whoa" by the driver. I could not catch my breath to yell, "Whoa!" for several seconds. By the time I did, Roda, the mule, had traveled about thirty feet, plow sliding along on the side behind the mule. That accident happened in the middle of a new field that had been planted in rows of corn. Later in the crop year, when the corn stalks were growing, two or three stalks were growing in the middle spaces between the rows of corn where the errant mule and plow had dragged a few seed out of the ground and replanted them.

One purpose plowing a new ground served, as described above, was to locate where the culprit roots were so they could be dug out, cut off with an axe, and relegated to the next brush heap for burning. Good job to consume a boy's time when it was raining or too wet to plow or do other necessary farmwork.

The first year, the turnips grew beautifully. Some of the neighbors who had helped clear the field were beneficiaries of good messes of turnips until spring. They were not the only ones to benefit from the work and crop. Any neighbor who let it be known that his/her turnip patch this winter was not up to par was fed from the bounty.

The second year was not as bad. The first spring the new ground was put to a crop was corn. Why not? The Indians had been growing corn in this manner for thousands of years, though the technological level of our archeology at the time of the Indians was yet to discover and make known this truth.

The digging and burning continued into the third and fourth years. By the fifth year, there remained only a couple of old heart pine stumps in the new ground, and the beloved cash crop of the South—king cotton—could be planted.

This was one of the years when the cotton variety of the red leaves was the rage. With short staple, the variety produced more lint per acre than the popular Delta Pine Land (DPL) varieties of the time, and the extra pounds of lint were expected to make up for the loss in price due to the shorter staple of fifteen-sixteenths to thirty-one thirty-secondths of an inch. Sometimes it was economic; sometimes it was not. Mr. Boll Weevil was still in the race and determined to be the winner. There were a few other varieties of cotton that could be chosen if one had the money with which to pay for it. I remember hogs being traded for cottonseed. One popular variety was called half-and-half because the picked cotton was supposed to yield about half its weight in lint and half in seed.

Who could foretell that this land clearing in the mid and late `30s, during the Great Depression, would prove to be the end of clearing land by hand as the day of the tractor, track hoe, backhoe, and bulldozer were on their way.

It was not an accident that there was still a legitimate argument in my college rooms near the LSU dairy barn in 1942 as to whether the mule was or was not superior to the tractor in getting the job done.

Who said we seemed to be a generation behind the times? Why not two generations? We were surviving with tools, the likes of which were used five hundred years earlier.

In the piney woods, it can still be done.

# CHAPTER 14
# Barn and Bridge Dances

Having fun on Saturday night was pursued during the Great Depression the same as other times. Housing was often log cabins or the first generation of sawmill shacks like the one we lived in.

Large buildings, public or private, with rooms large enough to provide a dance floor were scarce.

Wagon roads were gradually being converted into somewhat improved graveled roads across the countryside of the nation so the increasing numbers of automobiles and trucks could provide transportation to and from the railroads and bus stations.

I remember Marshall Rhodes, from Vowells Mill, Louisiana, walking five miles to the Sylvest house and spending the night about 1933. He and my brother Frank each had a guitar and played and sang gospel and country music. As they played and sang for practice, this eight-year-old little brother eavesdropped every opportunity he could get. I heard Marshall ask Frank if he would come play Saturday night at a bridge near Vowells Mill. I hardly knew where Vowells Mill was, at age eight, but I understood that there was to be a dance, it was going to be on a bridge, and a chicken fry was going to go along with it. Marshall and Frank were going to provide guitar music, and someone I did not know was going to play the fiddle.

As I grew older, the picture became clearer.

The choice place with a smooth enough wood surface, and a large enough area on which young people could dance, was a bridge on a gravel road. The young people made brush brooms of dogwood bushes and swept the gravel off the bridge in an area large enough for a few couples to dance. The musicians would set up on the edge of the bridge and the program was on.

Some walked to the bridge, if they lived close enough. If not, there was kind of a community effort on the part of all those few who had access to cars to give rides to those who did not. Often a collection was taken to pay for more gasoline so the cars could ramble more.

A girl who was pretty, or sang well, or both, was somewhat popular. This description included all the young ladies I knew. They could always attract some transportation.

Those were the days of the cars with running boards where all the passengers who could not get inside the vehicle could stand on the running boards and hold on to the frame of the car. Some cars even had exterior handles for that purpose.

Another popular feature on cars of that time was rumble seats. I even owned one of these popular little dudes as a novelty I could not afford when a college student later in life.

I remember a few of the marriages that followed these years.

Dixie Sylvest married Walter Moss Jr.

Coleman Foshee married Nezzie Nicholls.

Otis Booty married Carmel Burleson.

Spurgeon Sylvest married Netha Burleson.

D. Tynes married Daisy Burleson.

Curtis Rhodes married Hattie Kay.

Johnnie Kay married Orene Ryalls.

Eric Miller married Effie Foshee.

Elbert Foshee married Maureen Malone.

These people were young adults I loved when I was a little boy during the Great Depression. I was happy to think of them as being together forever.

I have forgotten the names of the other participants in that dance on the bridge. I never found out on which bridge it took place. The most likely bridge would be the one over Bayou de Muse near Vowells Mill, on the road that runs from Flora to Vowells Mill.

A bridge was sometimes the location of choice rather than the packed dirt floor of a barn. A barn was the choice location for a dance when rain and adverse weather interfered. Hence, I believe, the origin of the expression "barn dance."

The week following the bridge dance, I heard adult discussion about where the chickens came from that were fried on the creek bank that Saturday night. I got the impression that some of them had been donated and some of them had been taken from some parents' chicken house without permission.

The number of automobiles in the community gradually increased in the 1930s, and the roads were gradually improved.

The closest paved road to Provencal was LA 1 that went from Natchitoches to Alexandria and ran about eight miles east of Provencal. Most of that was paved in the 1930s and part of it, near Cloutierville, was not paved until the late 1940s.

## Candy Pulling

It was wintertime, and some of the young people who were away from their homes to go to college were at home for the holidays.

A candy pulling was planned at the Sylvest house. I remember that Johnnie Sylvest and Effie Foshee were participants. Syrup was provided by the farm. About ten young people showed up for the fun. Johnnie, my sister, was one of the cooks. Minnie Sylvest, my mother, was the supervisor. Open kettle cane syrup was poured into a saucepan and heated, cooked, and monitored closely to see whether it was thick enough to "pull." That meant that the syrup was not quite ready to crystallize, but if managed correctly by pulling, from one hand to the other so air was incorporated into the cooling syrup, it would turn lighter in color and when cooled would be delicious, brittle taffy-like candy.

The test for the right stage was an art. By practicing this method, the cook could become quite good at judging when the cooking syrup was ready. Dipping a bit of syrup with a spoon and letting it pour back into the pot left a drop on the edge of a spoon. That last drop would be dropped into a cup of cold water to see if it solidified or remained liquid. When it reached the point at which it thickened immediately upon hitting the water, it was done. If cooked beyond this point, it would turn to sugar. Minnie Sylvest was an expert in this process. Johnnie had become quite proficient at it as well.

When the syrup was judged to be "right," it was poured into baking tins. Hands were washed and greased with butter so the warm syrup would not stick to the hands. Everyone had to work fast to get the pulling done before the syrup cooled completely. There were about four baking tins in use, and two people would work the thickening syrup in each tin. If a girl could get her beau to join her, a bit of laughing and sparking could go on during the candy pulling. The resulting candy was a brittle taffy like syrup candy, which could have peanuts in it or be eaten like it was.

Two or more batches were often made. On occasion, I was asked to shell a gallon of peanuts the day before for use in mixing into cooked syrup to make peanut brittle.

Sometimes we took parched peanuts and shelled and husked them. Then we placed them in a ten-pound tin can and pounded them with a steel hammer made from the coupling pin of the old sawmill railroad train. Pounding, stirring, and pounding some more resulted in homemade peanut butter.

If enough food had not been provided already, there was an ample supply of popcorn grown on the farm which could be quickly popped and added to the candy party menu.

Popping popcorn was one of our favorite wintertime indoor activities. Usually parching peanuts went along at the same time.

I still think fondly of those activities and times in Provencal in the piney woods.

# CHAPTER 15
# The Family Dog

The lives of the piney woods homesteaders were much more intimately interwoven with the work animals, dogs, and other pets than has been the case for succeeding generations. We depended upon them for power and for protection.

The family dog was usually a general-purpose animal which was allowed to run freely about the place. Sometimes the yard fence was so secure around the house that the dog could not get out and roam at large. This was usually the case if neighbors lived nearby.

On the Sylvest farm, the dog could run freely as we were rather isolated, being a quarter of a mile from our closest neighbor, Henry McGaskey.

The family dog that I first remember was Fido, an all-black, semi-longhaired dog that was half collie and half cur. He was medium sized and was excellent in controlling hogs, cows, and goats and as a watchdog. What a fine pet as a bodyguard for children. We tried to ride Fido. We tried to hitch him to our red wagon. I am not sure we did not try to use him for a bed.

When I was eight years old, in 1933, John D had decided that Fido was getting old so it was time for us to get another dog and begin training it as a replacement. The new dog was a new all-black female with short hair that could have passed for a black Labrador retriever. We named the new dog Spyro.

Fido and Spyro made a beautiful pair and were great playmates for Ruth, six, Royce, three, and yours truly, age eight.

A mad dog (infected with hydrophobia) came into the neighborhood from toward Provencal and passed through our yard. He got into a fight with Fido and Spyro under our house. The strange dog then left the farm and went toward Vowells Mill.

Men of the community were aware of the dog, which appeared to be hydrophobic, as it exhibited the usual symptoms, and they were pursuing it as fast as they could. After we learned of the probability that the strange dog was mad, we chained our dogs so they could not depart.

The next day we learned that Mr. Ellis Honeycutt, one of our neighbors on the road from our house to Vowells Mill, had killed the offending dog. The Natchitoches Parish Health Department sent the head of the suspect dog to the laboratory in Shreveport. A telegram came back saying the dog tested positive for hydrophobia and all dogs that were known to have had contact with him should be destroyed. A committee of men of the community rode together and delivered this message and assisted the owners in disposing of their exposed dogs. John D and Spurgeon went with the committee, and they destroyed Fido and Spyro.

It was a sad time on the Sylvest homestead.

Many other homesteads were similarly affected.

New puppies became the rage, and we soon had a yellow puppy with a white ring around his neck. What did we name our new dog? Ring, of course. Ring was to be our family dog for sixteen years.

Ring was a good hog dog. A hog dog is one that has been trained to hunt and locate wild hogs in the woods. It is also trained to drive the hogs, lead them, and otherwise herd them to the pen spot or area you direct them to go.

Tommy, eldest son, recently asked me how we trained our dogs. I was dumbfounded with the question.

Nothing wrong with the question. Just, to this octogenarian, the answer was so obvious that I had never thought about an answer to the question. After all, didn't every family have a hog dog, and didn't every family member know how that dog had been trained?

Not so in the twenty-first century.

So, put on your thinking cap, and let's see what you can do with this one, oldie!

First, we've got to get the puppy with the desired parentage so there will be a good chance the genes are in place to increase our chances of getting a really good hog dog. Speak for the puppy about as soon as the litter is old enough for the puppies to open their eyes. Select the one from the litter that you and the owner of the female dog can agree upon. The puppies will open their eyes when they are about nine days old.

During that time, they are feasting on their mother's milk. This is of extreme importance, as they must get the full benefit of drinking the colostrum, the first milk of the mother that has just given birth to the litter. For about two weeks, the mother continues to give milk high in antibodies, which the young pups must have to give them immunity from many of the most common diseases of canines.

When the pup is about six weeks old, it is old enough to leave its mother and be fed by a new owner who knows how to care for it.

At our place, there was always plenty of milk so Ring, as a little pup, was fed all the cow's milk he could drink every day of his life. When he was a bit older, we began to give him cooked eggs and meat to keep his diet high in protein.

Ring grew well and within six months would wait for the school bus to meet his young masters and playmates after school, which became his favorite playtime.

Spurgeon, an older brother, took charge of training Ring. He led him in chasing hogs and had him follow and bark at cows and mules. A puppy will run wherever you run if you are playing with it.

By the time Ring was a year old, Spurgeon took him to hunt hogs with Jefferson Masters, who had a good mature and experienced hog dog. Only a few times of this and Ring was getting better every day at being a good hog dog.

Ruth, Royce, and I saw to it that Ring was becoming a good playmate.

We all taught Ring to bark at anything and anybody who was strange to our homestead. The protocol for a family dog was to bark at whomever approached the homestead and make them stop at the gate of the yard fence. If an adult member of the household commanded Ring to shut up, he would cease barking and go back to his bed under the house. This is one of the first commands a new puppy learns.

At the Sylvest homestead, another of the first lessons for a young puppy is that it is never, but never, to come upon the porch of the house, let alone into the room of the house. The lesson is you are a dog and your place is anywhere but inside the house. This was taught during the first few weeks of its life by switching it with a keen little switch every time it as much as gets on a step toward going onto the porch or into the house. By the time it is six months old, it will know the lesson, never to be forgotten.

Our neighbors, by and large did not have such a rule for their dogs. They were always amazed that our dogs were yard dogs, not housedogs, and that the dogs knew it.

In the process of the dog's growing up, he was taught standard commands, which all family members knew. "Git him," was the command for the dog to chase whatever it was being directed to go after.

"Here, Ring," was the command to come to the caller if the caller persisted in calling. "Here, Ring," was used to command the dog to cease chasing whatever it might be chasing as well.

In order to emphasize any command, it was repeated a few times.

There were characteristic whistles which were used to command dogs a long distance from the owner. A long whistle made with the lips first with a low pitch followed by and rising immediately to a high pitch was the signal for the dog to come to the whistling master.

This was a loud whistle as voice commands were used more for directing the dogs when they were close to person giving the command.

To indicate urgency, the whistle was repeated rapidly. When this was done, the trained dog came running to the caller with great haste.

I remember one time I was in the corncrib shucking and shelling corn to take to the gristmill. That was kind of a lonesome job. A hog which was in the pasture surrounding the corncrib had come under the barn and was getting into a location where it was going to interfere with the chickens I was feeding corn.

Just the time for a dog. At the time, we had a female dog named Tag. Tag was pregnant, in the latter stages. I called Tag. Tag came running from the potato house where she made her bed. Her route to the corncrib where I was calling was to go about fifty yards down the pasture fence and jump over a low spot in the fence.

Tag came running with her big puppy-filled belly just waddling. When she got to the fence where she had to jump, she stopped and turned and started back toward the potato house. When she did this, I increased the urgency of my whistling and calling. Tag turned around again and ran to the low spot in the fence. I was watching her. When she jumped over the fence, a baby puppy fell out of her and hit the ground. Tag immediately ignored my calling, picked up the puppy in her mouth, jumped back over the fence with the puppy in her mouth, and carried the puppy back behind our home a hundred yards to the potato house.

I was some excited. I interrupted my corn shucking and shelling chore to go observe the birthing of nine baby puppies. Yes, kids who grew up in the piney woods with all their animals during the Great Depression learned many life lessons.

Rapid, high-pitched whistles uttered in succession were the command to go after whatever was the subject. This was the equivalent of "get him." It was useful at a greater distance.

Nearly all homesteads had a cow horn, carved into a "hunting horn," which their dogs were trained to come to when it was blown repeatedly. Called simply "the horn" at our house, it was kept over the fireplace mantel in the living room, where a double-barreled shotgun also resided.

The cow horn was used not only to call the dog but for other signals. For example, my mother blew the cow horn when it was time for the men working in the field to leave their work and come to dinner at the house. It gave them enough time walk to the house, wash and dry their hands at the well at 12:00 noon, and come sit at the table.

The horn could be heard by a dog for up to a mile. A man could hear the horn for half a mile.

All adult male members of the household were charged with learning to blow the horn in case they needed to know how to announce an emergency. Some of the ladies also learned how to blow the horn.

If an emergency occurred, such as a fire, the horn was to be blown three times. After a good long wait, it was to be blown three more times. This was a well-known signal known by all members of the households in the piney woods during the 1930s.

When I was attending LSU in the 1940s, after WW II, I would hitchhike to Provencal from Baton Rouge. Most frequently, I would have to walk the last mile to our homestead, and this would be in the middle of the night.

I found I could never get in the house without my mother being awake. Who wants to awaken their mother at 1:00 a.m.? I realized the reason I could not get into the house without her hearing me was that Ring, the family dog, barked when I was about a half mile away from the house and my mother heard the barking dog and knew something was amiss.

I decided to outfox that dog. One time, when I was a half mile from the house, I called Ring. Happy to hear his old playmate's voice, Ring came to meet me and quietly accompanied me to the house without a bark. I went inside. Our house was never locked. I went to bed and went to sleep. That is where Minnie found me when she awakened in the morning. Considerably alarmed that anyone could possibly get into that house in the middle of the night without her knowing it, she was somewhat relieved when I told her what I had done.

Yes, sir, with a good family dog like Ring, Minnie and John D were safe sleeping in that house with the doors unlocked. Ring could be depended upon to announce all strange visitors and stop them before they got inside. Equally protected by their family dog were all the other homesteaders of the piney woods during the Great Depression of the 1930s.

I remember Fido and Ring fondly.

How do you train a dog? Indeed!

How does a man train a boy?

Let him grow up beside a man.

# CHAPTER 16
# The Dairy Business

In 1928, the price of cream for butterfat was high. John D and Minnie decided to go into the dairy business at Provencal.

A truck from a creamery passed down the Hagewood-Leesville Highway only one mile from the Sylvest homestead regularly to pick up cans of cream, perhaps twice per week.

The economic factors seemed to be in place to make this a workable and profitable farm enterprise.

Siblings who lived in Washington Parish had been in the dairy business for years, so dairying was no strange farm enterprise to John D and Minnie Sylvest. John D's brother, Thomas Christopher, for whom I was named, was milking cows south of Franklinton, Louisiana. Esco Fendlason, brother to Minnie, was milking cows at Sunny Hill, Louisiana, west of Franklinton.

With no difficulty mortgaging the farm, John D was able to get a bank loan, with which he purchased a herd of dairy cows and the equipment to process the milk.

My earliest memory of this operation is of my brothers, Frankie and Spurgeon, feeding and milking the cows and separating the cream from the milk with a hand-cranked de Laval milk separator.

The Board of Health required a screened-in milk processing room in which the milk and cream separation process was to take place. A small milk room about ten feet square with screen doors was built behind our house and the milk separator was installed. I remember that the lumber was planed pine boards. I had not seen much newly planed raw pine lumber in my young life. It was pretty. I recall that the "milk house," as it was called, was not painted. The planed lumber was just allowed to weather to the natural gray, bleached appearance.

I cannot remember the number of cows that were purchased, but I remember many of their names, like a black cow named Muley because, like a mule, she was naturally without horns. There was a part Longhorn, dun-colored cow named Pink with a beautiful set of horns, a Jersey cow named Brownie with very sharp horns. She was mean as the dickens, so mean that John D took a handsaw and sawed her horns off. We had a Jersey cow named Dot, so named after the cow in my first-grade reader, and a prized Jersey bull whose name I do not recall.

When Frankie and Spurgeon Sylvest, two of my older brothers, milked the cows, they poured the milk into ten-gallon cans which they hauled to the milk room on a two-wheeled cart built for that purpose. The milk was poured into a milk bucket which could be lifted to the height of five feet to pour it into the five-gallon container atop the milk separator. When the milk ran down into the separator, the long-handled crank was turned and the milk and cream were separated from each other by centrifugal force. The cream rose to the top of the spinning funnel-shaped plates and exited from a spout into a small can. The milk exited from a spout below the cream spout, as milk and cream separated by the force of the centrifuge and gravity. The skim milk was a much larger portion of the separation process, so it was collected in a larger can.

The separated cream, which was probably 30 percent butterfat, was kept aside and cooled by setting the cans containing it in a wooden trough and pouring cool well water around the cans. On "cream run" day, the five-gallon cans of cream were delivered to the highway by wagon to be hauled to the creamery to make butter. The truck was equipped with a scale and the farmer was given a receipt for the amount of cream he delivered to the truck. As I recall, during this brief period, John D received a check each month for the pounds of butterfat he had delivered. Without refrigeration, the product we sold was sour cream for the manufacture of butter.

Calamity seemed to follow calamity during the Depression years.

I remember, during the fall of that year, after cane grinding and syrup making season was over, our syrup evaporator pan was left with water in it. Without his intent, and before John D realized it, some of his dairy cattle, which had been turned loose to forage in the field where the syrup evaporator pan was located, had consumed some of the sweet, fermented water from the evaporator pan. Within forty-eight hours, the prize Jersey bull and some of the cows were dead from being poisoned by the fermented, contaminated water. The dead carcasses smelled terrible, and the fires to burn them lasted for weeks.

The dairy activity continued for a few weeks on a diminished scale until the price of cream suddenly declined from about forty cents a pound for butterfat to five cents per pound. The creamery truck stopped coming for the cream, and all dairy farmers were immediately out of business.

As I grew up, during my school years of 1931 to 1942, the milk house and separator fell into decay and only remained a monument to the memory. John D and Minnie retained the mortgage on the farm as their memento to their foray into the dairy business.

Interest was paid on that mortgage each year. The principal remained unpaid until WW II began on December 7, 1941, with the Japanese bombing of Pearl Harbor in Honolulu, Hawaii.

As I grew up, the cloud of that debt hung over the heads of my parents. I recall asking John D in 1942, upon their celebrating, with some fanfare, the paying off of the mortgage, "Papa, how much was the amount of the loan?"

As a sixteen-year-old, I almost cried in front of my parents over the agony they had to have gone through for over ten years when he told me the mortgage was for only three hundred dollars. That was the amount on which they could not raise enough money to make any payments more than the required interest annually. I walked away, to where they could not see me, and cried.

I do not know the rate of interest on that mortgage, but I still have it on my list of things to do, someday, to go to the Natchitoches Parish Courthouse to the Clerk of Court's Office to look up that mortgage in the register of mortgages just to see.

I do remember that John D borrowed money in the springtime one year to "make a crop with," probably one hundred dollars to buy seed and fertilizer. That principal of one hundred dollars carried an interest rate of 20 percent and was to be paid back when the cotton was ginned in the fall, about October 31. Years later, when I became a banker, I thought of that loan and realized that he had used the hundred dollars for about eight months and paid interest of twenty dollars, for an effective annual rate of closer to 30 percent.

Maybe one of our seven children will be so curious that they will look up the mortgage record and interest rate someday and share the facts with us all.

Of such experiences was the triumph over tragedy on the piney woods subsistence farm of the Sylvests of Provencal and of the millions of similar farms that were spread all over the rural South during the Great Depression.

We were never in danger of starving on the Sylvest farm, but the lack of money, currency of any kind with which to purchase anything, during the Depression years of the 1930s left its indelible mark on every one of us.

I know. I was there.

# CHAPTER 17
# A New Wood Stove

In the early 1930s, Artie, one of my older sisters, ordered a new wood-burning stove for the Sylvest homestead near Provencal. She was employed by the state of Louisiana at East Louisiana State Hospital at Jackson, having studied home economics at Louisiana State Normal College (presently Northwestern Louisiana University in Natchitoches, Louisiana) for a two-year certificate and was employed as a dietitian at the state's largest mental institution.

From that employment, Artie acquired the income to pay for a new stove. She placed the order by mail to Sears Roebuck and Company with instructions that the stove would be shipped by train to John D Sylvest at Provencal, Louisiana.

During those years, we received our mail at general delivery at the Provencal, Louisiana, post office. That meant that we had to go six miles to get our mail. During the school year, that requirement was commonly met by one of the schoolchildren riding to school in Provencal on the school transfer (bus), getting permission to leave the school grounds during the noon hour, and then walking the few blocks to the post office to get the mail.

A mail notice came informing us that there was a shipment from Sears Roebuck (no longer Roebuck) by freight to John D Sylvest and advising that we should check for it at the train depot.

There we discovered the stove as promised.

A trip to Provencal with our wagon was arranged. Older male members of the household accompanied John D to load and haul the stove to our house. The adults installed the stove, and I remember the conversation. There was a seventeen-inch wood box on the new stove, much longer than on the older stove, so we could now cut stove wood longer than before.

For some strange reason, there seemed to be more activity around the wood yard than before. I guess cutting stove wood suddenly seemed like an adventure. Believe me: before I finished high school and left the old homestead, I would find out that cutting and splitting cords of stove wood of any length was not an adventure but a backbreaking chore.

I spent many hours on one end of a crosscut saw with Frankie on the other, setting aside two or three cords of wood each summer for use the following year. Later, as Royce, five years younger than I, grew up a bit, he became my crosscut saw partner. That little brother began spending many hours pulling that crosscut saw when he was only ten years old. I know, because I was only fifteen at the time and he and I cut all the wood.

Cutting and splitting stove wood is hard work for grown men, let alone little kids. We did what was required.

No one commented at the time of the new stove arrival about a block of wood sixteen inches long rather than fourteen inches long being harder to split. By the time I finished high school, both my experience and my mathematics were adequate to figure that out.

The stovetop of the new stove was much larger than the old one. This provided more working space for the cook, usually my mother or my sisters. Further, it sported a new feature. At the back of the stove behind the firebox and stovepipe was a ten-gallon tank of galvanized metal, which would contain water for heating. On the old stove, the choices for heating water were to put a pan of water on top of the stove or put the black cast-iron kettle on top of the stove where one stove-eye had been removed. Yes, we had what we called a stove-eye lifter with which we could remove a round piece of the stovetop called an eye. The bottom of the black cast-iron kettle was shaped and fitted to fit in the hole where stove eyes had been removed for the purpose. The purpose for removing the stove eye and placing the kettle there was to get the kettle closer to the heat of the fire in the stove firebox. That reduced the time and the amount of wood required to heat water for the many purposes for which warm or hot water was desirable. Bathing, washing dishes, pots and pans, and on and on.

I did not understand the magnitude of what a better stove could do to improve the life of the cook, but I did understand that more sweet potatoes or peanuts could be cooked in the new larger oven at one time.

As I grew older, I learned to give thanks for my older siblings who assisted my parents in meeting the needs of the younger children both physically doing hard work and financially with a few dollars at critical times during the Depression.

I have difficulty writing about the shortage of money during the Great Depression without implying that we were so poverty stricken that we were in danger of starving. Being short of cash was not closely connected with any threat of starving. I only remember one time when we did not have all the bread all members of the household could consume. That time lasted for only two weeks and while without bread, corn meal, or flour, we had adequate meat, vegetables, cane syrup, potatoes, milk, and eggs for everyone to be well nourished.

Sometimes we would go without fresh greens for weeks. In that case, we usually had plenty of canned fruit, and on and on. Or we would run out of syrup but the grinding season would be only three weeks away.

I remember that the new stove kept the whole kitchen warmer in the wintertime.

For about three years, until the galvanized water tank on the stove sprang a leak from rusting, we enjoyed more ready warm or hot water than we had ever had before. More baths. Cleaner kids!

I remember my mother's relief when she got an electric stove nearly twenty years later and no longer had to be concerned about stove wood.

# CHAPTER 18
# Wagon Roads, Bridle Paths, and Trails

As soon as I was big enough and old enough to be allowed to play about two hundred yards from our house, I discovered that there were interesting paths that were traveled by people moving about the community. Only a few of these travelers were able to move about by motorized vehicle. Most such vehicles in the early 1920s and 30s were Ford Model T autos and trucks.

Even these were so rare that I would like to leave them for treatment in another section.

Wagons were the primary means of getting from one place to another if the family was to accompany the driver or loads of any kind were to be transported. The most common wagon was four wheeled and of a size to be pulled by two draft animals: horses or, most commonly, mules, and occasionally a mixture of the two.

Such a wagon was called a "double wagon," meaning it was intended and was of a size to be pulled by two draft animals. The front of the wagon to which the team was hitched had a timber about ten feet long extending in front called a tongue. One mule was harnessed and hitched to a doubletree and singletree on each side of the tongue.

The harnesses were fastened together in front of the team at the end of the tongue and held together by a breast yoke. A breast yoke was a wooden device about five feet long with rings, chains, and hooks on each end to attach to the tongue of the wagon and to the harness of each mule.

In this way, the wagon was guided by the teamster or driver by guiding the mules with driving lines for reins. Typically, driving lines were made of leather straps about one inch wide and nearly one-quarter inch thick, stitched and riveted into a configuration to fit through rings on the harness and on to the bits of the mules.

To someone familiar with this equipment, it sounds ridiculous to describe it in such detail.

However, let me assure you that, as early as 1943, I recall an agricultural student at LSU named Draper coming to the dairy barn where we used a one-mule cart to haul manure to store in a corner of the barnyard to be used later for fertilization of the pastures. Draper grew up in the city of New Orleans where horse-drawn vehicles were not as common anymore, and he could not recall the name of the gear we put on the mule to control the mule and enable the mule to pull the cart. When Draper asked Jack Stanley and me to put the "stuff" on the mule, Jack and I howled with laughter. Jack asked Draper if he was talking about the "harness," and Draper said, "Yes, that's it, the harness." More roaring laughter. Such hilarious comedy.

Jack and I were thoroughly entertained by the idea that anyone could live to be a grown man during those years and not know what the word *harness* was.

One could wonder where ignorance existed, how it is to be defined, and who, if anyone, had a monopoly on it: Draper or Jack and me.

So much for the double wagon.

Just as common in the 1930s was the one-horse wagon constructed of lighter material than the double wagon and designed that way to be pulled by one draft animal, either horse or mule.

The one-horse wagon did not have a tongue in front but a pair of shafts between which the horse to pull the wagon was hitched. This was the same arrangement used on buggies to enable the harnessing of the draft animal to the wheeled vehicle it was to pull.

From the paragraphs above, one can appreciate the significance of the term "one-horse" referring to a smaller version of anything. Hence, if a farmer had a small farm, it was simply referred to as a "one-horse" farm or a "one-horse" operation contrasted to a larger version of the same object whether it be a farm, business, store, or other entity.

Additional horse-drawn units were a carriage and a surrey, which were designed to be pulled by a pair of draft animals. These were not common in the section of piney woods around Provencal. They were scarce because the typical rural resident was owner or tenant on a small piece of land and could not afford a two-horse vehicle let alone a classier version of one, such as the surrey or carriage. I recall that we had only Mr. Steve Roberts, one neighbor, who owned and commonly used a surrey. Mr. Roberts used the surrey to attend church with his wife at Harmony Baptist Church about four miles southeast of Provencal.

There were few buggies, because they were not a multipurpose, horse-drawn vehicle. Instead, they were especially designed to convey persons across the countryside rapidly and with minimum strain on the draft animal. A good, fast buggy horse was a treasure to the owner of a buggy. We had a buggy and a buggy horse when I was preschool, but it was used for my older siblings to drive to school. The gasoline powered school "transfers" were not provided to transport children to school until the late 1920s. The buggy most commonly observed belonged to Dr. Addison, an MD who lived in Provencal. Dr. Addison traveled in a buggy for miles around Provencal in his practice of medicine. Another buggy I remember was owned and driven by Mr. John Wagley, the senior member of a prominent family that lived near Provencal. If my memory serves me well, Mr. Wagley was a veteran of the Civil War, often referred to as the War Between the States when I was a child in the 1920s and 1930s.

As I grew older, I played with siblings and friends in the old wagon roads which were still clearly visible throughout the piney woods as old roads which had been heavily traveled early in the twentieth century by travelers moving westward to Texas and points farther west.

As a teenager in the 1930s, I was familiar with dozens of sites of old crossings, fiords, and bridges on the creeks and smaller streams which characterized the woodlands of the Kisatchie National Forest. Our residence was in what had been named the no-man's-land because it was land between the Red River and the Sabine River claimed by both Spain and the United States for years after the Louisiana Purchase in the early nineteenth century.

I am confident I could take an observer today back to the same spots and find remnants of some of the "cuts" through hillsides where the sheer number of wagon wheels which had rolled over the spot and the resulting erosion left pathways with walls several feet high and a width of only slightly more than the minimum necessary for a wagon to pass that way.

So, wagon paths that led east and west were common, much more common than ones leading north and south.

Not all paths were wide enough for wagons. Some of them led for miles through the forested hills which were only wide enough for a rider on a horse or mule to pass.

These paths grew from usage. Typically, a bridle path went along ridges which were not too muddy or too steep. In their routing, they led past springs of good drinking water, which were required by all travelers and their animals.

I recall that on the road that extended from Provencal to Vowells Mill, there was a trail that paralleled Horse Pen Creek. This trail crossed the Provencal-Vowells Mill Road at a cemetery named Cedron and led into the woods in the direction of Robeline. It was a bridle path used by mounted travelers and travelers who were traveling afoot. A church, no longer there in the 1930s, had been located nearby and the cemetery was the remaining artifact. When I was a small child in the 1920s or 1930s, I accompanied my mother and siblings to a "graveyard working" at that old Cedron cemetery. Many of our neighbors had deceased relatives buried there.

I recall that my mother showed me a block of wood about fifteen inches high and told me that it was a "mounting block." That was a block used by anyone who needed it to climb upon to make mounting their horse or mule easier. It was used mostly for ladies and children.

I remember sitting on the mounting block and imagining all of those who had used the block to get on a horse.

Buggy owners used wagon roads. However, I remember that the private road near the house of a buggy owner always had three little footpaths rather than the two only on such a road to the house of a double-wagon owner. That difference fascinated me and led to many questions from me directed to my dad about horses, mules, wagons buggies, and automobiles. In the case of the double wagon, the roadway had only two trails because the horse on the right side of the wagon walked where the right wheels would pass and wear out a trail. The same on the left side of the wagon and the road.

In the case of the single wagon or buggy, the horse walked in the middle of the roadway, making a trail with his feet while two more trails were made in the buggy road by the wheels of the buggy, hence a road with three paths and grass growing in between.

At certain locations on the major streams, such as where wagon roads crossed the creeks, there were bridges. One such bridge was over McKim's Creek on the Sylvest homestead. I recall watching my dad and brothers repair the bridge. At the time, I was too young and small to be of much help. The bridge was on a wagon road which led from Henry McGaskey's gristmill and home south to Antioch Church and cemetery, an institution used by blacks only during the 1930s.

I recall that Royce and Ralph Sylvest, my younger brother and nephew, respectively, cut wood from our homestead during the early 1940s and hauled it to Antioch Church and school so the patrons, teachers, and students would have firewood during cold weather. This was done for no pay. It was just what neighbors did to help each other. Not many black families had wagons on which to haul wood. They often had to borrow a mule to pull a slide to move wood to their yard.

This cooperative activity was typical of a working arrangement common between nearly all of the families of the piney woods communities during the Great Depression.

Wagon roads through the woods were typically laid out by the travelers, without surveying instruments. When a wagon road became so rough from eroded ruts that it could no longer be traversed by the wagon and team, someone had to take action.

Usually an axe was all that was required. One member of the traveling party would scout out another route over which the wagon and teams could travel, cut the smallest trees and bushes, and drive the team over the new route. In time and as the level traffic determined, the road followed the rerouted path.

I recall that in certain spots on these wagon roads, the path would lead between large trees. Sometimes in these spots, the path would become so eroded that the roots of the trees beside the road were exposed, and when the wagon wheel rolled over them, it was a rough bump to any passengers in the wagon and threatened to damage the wagon itself. When this occurred, it could become an emergency which was addressed by a local group of residents from several miles around agreeing to have a "work day" on which the able-bodied members of the affected families would assemble at a certain spot on the road at the appointed time, agree on who was to direct the operation, and go to work with axes, shovels, and hoes, plus horse-drawn equipment as available and called for. At noontime, teenagers on horse or mule or foot would show up with buckets filled with fried ham and bacon, biscuits, cornbread, baked sweet potatoes, and whatever other dishes the ladies at home had prepared for their men folk. Such work had to be done when the weather was suitable. This was traditionally done after crops were planted in the spring and before the harvest began in earnest in the fall. Or she saying was, "We are going to have a road working on Monday, the fifth of July, after everybody has laid by (plowed and hoed the cotton crop for the last time)."

Some of these trees and bushes were not cut off near ground level and some of them were fairly large, a foot or more in diameter, so the remaining stump might be as tall as twelve inches and be right in the middle of the road. This is because the wheels were four feet or more in diameter; hence, the axles would easily clear a foot tall stump in the road. This caused a problem when these same roads, unimproved, began to be used occasionally by motorized vehicles which were much closer to the ground. I often saw travelers have to stop, get their axe or saw out of their vehicle, and trim or cut down a stump so their car could go over it.

Later, some of these wagon roads and trails were surveyed by the parish and state governments, graded and/or graveled, and even hard-surfaced to become local roads or state highways. Some of the local roads, like Sylvest Road, were not actually surveyed but were simply cleared out by axe, shovel, horse-drawn slip, and gasoline-powered grader. They became public property by virtue of the fact that the police jury, the parish governing body, took possession of the right of way by clearing, grading, adding gravel in muddy stretches, and maybe even as long as twenty-five or forty years later pouring asphalt strips wide enough to accommodate a vehicle right up to the front of a residence surrounded by woods and fields.

Louisiana Highway 117, from Hagewood to Leesville, is one such road. Now, about eighty years later, it is a hard-surfaced connection between two county seats, Leesville of Vernon Parish and Natchitoches of Natchitoches Parish.

# CHAPTER 19
# Safety in the Piney Woods

As one can imagine, when our country, the United States of America, had a population of only 130 million people in 1931, when I started to school, and over half of that population was rural, many of the families lived on pieces of land scattered over the rural regions of forty-eight states with their nearest neighbor over a mile away. This characteristic of our population dispersion grew from the availability of land. Since the federal government did not have an income tax system until about 1912, its revenue was limited. Hence, disposing of the federal lands by homesteading and sale, and by selling the produce there from myriad ways, was the primary source of income for the national government.

This feature of the population distribution had left many of the homesteaders and pioneers of the generations immediately preceding to the Great Depression exposed to foul play from Indians, outlaws, and wildlife.

Addressing this isolation and protecting the homebound members of the family, wives and children, elderly and ill when the head of the household and all the able-bodied members of the family were out in the fields working, had to be addressed by each family.

First, every family had a shotgun and/or rifle, and all men, women, and children members of the household from about age twelve upward were trained to use all the guns of the house. It just went with the territory. This account might provide a bit of background information to some of the younger and more urban portions of our population who do not understand the views of the gun lobbies at all.

Sequentially, the way safety and security was addressed when a new family settled on a new homestead, or piece of land acquired by trade, purchase, etc., was, upon arrival, prop your gun on a nearby tree where it is easily accessible while you are unloading enough of your possessions from ox cart, canoe, or whatever. Do not allow yourself to be approached by one or more armed strangers without being where you could reach your gun.

This configuration and state of alertness was maintained during the construction of the initial dwelling.

Typically, family groups would relocate together so there was some safety in numbers. Large families were the norm. There were often a man and wife with some small children, a grown offspring who may be married, and grown sons and/or daughters who joined in the common family effort.

In this way, not only was the safety element addressed and shared but other resources from food to labor and skills were as well.

Sometimes two houses were built on adjacent sites so the same water source, perhaps a spring, could be shared. The spring in question might be far enough from the two homesites that it could also be accessed by the general public passing by. Not every single homesite had the luxury of its own spring or well.

The comparatively rare spring that ran for year after year was not usually fenced in by one family, but the trail or wagon road running nearby went right past the spring so it could be reached for water as needed. It was assumed to be a public resource.

After the selection of the homesite, the construction of the shelter and accessory structures was addressed. Appropriate drainage, distances apart, sizes of buildings to be built, and choice of building materials available were weighed.

Security was never left out of these evaluations.

Any family member of enough maturity not only learned how to operate a firearm but could use all the basic hand tools of the pioneer.

One device each family had was a hunting horn, not only used to control dogs but to be blown by family members for other communication purposes. Some of these were to announce emergencies, be it a fire, accident, illness, or other life-threatening need.

Minnie, my mother, blew our hunting horn in the 1930s at noon each day so the rest of the family in hearing distance knew it was noon and time to come to the house to "wash up" and eat.

Any family member might blow that horn to call our dog from anywhere in hearing distance. For example, a strange bull might come from the nearby range and break the fence and get into the garden where it was eating all the vegetables. A human being must be cautious about approaching a strange bull which is more likely to run after you than from you. Ideal solution, blow the horn for the dog and sic the dog on the bull, hog, or whatever.

All family dogs were trained to chase away all animals that were out of place. They even knew to bark to announce that the out of place animal was indeed out of place, so appropriate and timely action could be taken.

How about approaching strangers and only the mother and a baby are at home, very vulnerable to foul play? To avoid this kind of circumstance, plans have been the norm from before the time the relocation was made.

Often the first thing built upon arrival at a new location was a fenced in area so the milk cow's calf could be penned within an enclosure. In this manner, the milk cow would not ramble so far that she could not be found and milked. That consideration was typically one of the first to be addressed. Prior to penning the calf, the calf might even be tied with a rope to a tree so the mother stays nearby until a pen for the calf is built.

Often some members of the family group preceded the others, the advance party going ahead to build a pen for cows, horses, etc. and a shelter to be used during home construction period before the other family members are brought to the new location.

One structure which nearly always was built early in the process was a fence surrounding the residence site. If the new site was particularly remote, the fence was often built before the residence.

The power of the fence as a barrier is immense. Not only does it prevent a person from physically approaching the residence without coming through the fence, but it speaks volumes by its presence about the territory inside that fence being "mine" and anyone entering that arena does so only with my permission. The fence denotes possession of property rights, a cultural characteristic brought from Europe by our ancestors. It was not a part of the common culture of the Native Americans, who regarded real property as public domain.

More specifically and practically, it was a defensible boundary. Inside every new fenced-in area resided a family dog. I remember when the yard of every neighbor was fenced in by a picket fence. Entering a single one of our neighbors' yards without the owners' permission just was not done. When I approached the house of a neighbor as a teenager, I stopped at the gate to the yard and watched with skepticism the family dog as it barked at me from inside the yard. The typical confrontation went something like this.

Willie Foshee's dog Youno barks at me. I am afraid he will bite me if I walk through the gate, so I just stand outside the gate waiting for a family member to come speak to Youno. Mrs. Foshee (Miss Algie) comes to the front door and says, "Shut up, Youno. Come on in, Ard, he will leave you alone."

When Miss Algie said, "Shut up, Youno," the dog immediately quit barking and went under the house. I walked into the yard and entered the house.

This fence and dog arrangement was not accidental. It was purposeful and almost universal in the piney woods of South during the Great Depression, even in the villages like Provencal, which had a population of about eight hundred. What is now the city of Natchitoches, the county seat of Natchitoches Parish, had a population of just over 5,000 in 1930.

The typical house was made of wood sawed in the early 1900s when the virgin pine forests of the South were logged completely. Almost no stands of virgin pine timber remain in our state.

The typical fence surrounding one of these houses was made of split pickets. Pickets were rived out of pine or oak timber, depending upon what was available at the time. White oak, which splits easily with a froe, was most commonly used when available, and the standard length of yard-fence pickets was six feet. The lathe, or cross pieces to which pickets were nailed, were usually about eight feet long. Two were nailed horizontally to fat pine posts set in the ground about eight feet apart.

One lathe was nailed about fifteen inches from the ground, and the other about four feet from the ground. With this design, the watchdog inside the fence could not climb the fence and abandon his assigned duty as a watchdog.

Such a fence would keep out all the farm animals and keep the family dog inside the fence. The idea of keeping the guard dog inside the fence was for the dog to defend the territory, to keep everyone out except those who were invited in.

With such a fence, and such a dog, and the typical gun owned by the household, the family felt secure.

If the man of the house was to be gone from home overnight or more, it was typical for a relative who lived nearby or a neighbor to come spend the night with a lone wife or mother with small children.

Noise pollution had not arrived. The noises of the remote homestead included a variety of characteristic sounds. Roosters crowed, particularly near daybreak, just before sunrise. Cows *mooed* just before milking time in the morning and in the evening. The calves *baaed* in reply to the *mooing* of their mothers. Birds sang from daybreak until sundown, purple martins in our birdhouses in the spring and northern mockingbirds day and night twelve months of the year. To this day, a most rewarding sound.

Sometimes a bull would bellow a very distinct and recognizable sound. Sometimes a mule would bray, the call of a jackass. Other times a horse would whinny.

At 7:00 a.m., the steam whistle of the Weaver Brothers Sawmill at Flora, Louisiana, would blow.

It would blow again at 12:00 noon and at 5:00 p.m. We used this whistle as the source of time to set our manually wound alarm clocks.

On school days, the exhaust whistle of Ernest Bell's school bus could be heard from about three miles away as Mr. Bell drove from Provencal the six miles to our house to pick up a load of us schoolchildren.

Often the dog would bark. Each dog had a pattern of barking signaling different types of disturbances. The bark of a dog to announce that a stranger is approaching the gate is a completely different bark from the same dog chasing a hog out of your garden. All members of the family knew the differences of the family dog's bark. We weren't taught these differences. We just kind of absorbed them by osmosis. Learning that was kind of like learning that when the sun comes up; daylight will enable you to see. You just did.

The centerpiece of our safety and security at our home during the Great Depression was our family dog.

Every family had one.

# CHAPTER 20
# Daily Meals

The selection of food to be served at meals on a given day on the old homestead was an ongoing process and subject to change based on to whom the meals were to be served, what foodstuffs were available, and how far in advance Minnie, the chief food preparer, had access to the described information.

Of course, the preferences of the family members and guests were of importance and were taken into consideration. However, the final result always had to fit within the limits of what was available.

The typical day during the Great Depression, Frank, my older brother, got out of bed first, about 4:30 a.m., before daybreak, and went to the kitchen to cook breakfast, as our mother's health was not good. Frank was still single and lived "at home," meaning in the household of his parents along with his parents and his three younger siblings: Ruth, Royce, and me.

Cooking breakfast meant cooking biscuits for the household, frying sugar-cured bacon, and frying chopped potatoes in cubes of about half an inch in size with eggs in the fat left over from cooking the bacon. This was actually a potato omelet and makes quite a good meal by itself. These delicacies were served on the dining table, which had, ever present, pitchers of whole milk, cream, butter, and home-cooked sugarcane syrup.

More than one large rectangular baking tin was required to hold enough biscuits for the breakfast meal. Typically, a large rectangular pan plus one round cake tin were required. This included enough biscuits for schoolchildren to take two each, slap a couple of pieces of home-cured bacon between the halves, roll them in a piece of newspaper, put them in a small paper bag, if a bag was available, and take them to school for lunch.

School lunches paid for by tax money did not begin in Natchitoches Parish until about 1938, and for the first two or three years they were available, Ruth, Royce, and I did not participate because we did not have the five cents per meal required to participate in the program. Instead, we took a lunch from home. Often a baked sweet potato was part of lunch we took from home. Occasionally, a boiled egg went into the bag. We carried the brown paper bag back home so it could be reused.

Often in the wintertime, we would have oatmeal for breakfast. It was accompanied by generous servings of fresh cream, butter, and milk. If we had refined sugar, which was most of the time, we put sugar on the oatmeal. Otherwise, we poured cane syrup on it. Sometimes we had grits served with butter, bacon, and biscuits.

The noon meal then became a matter of preparing enough for John D, Minnie, and Frank to eat and cooking enough of the major dishes that we could use it for the foundation dishes for the supper meal, the third meal of the day, which would again include the three schoolchildren.

After breakfast, someone, usually Minnie, would gather enough black-eyed peas from the garden to shell and produce a gallon for cooking. Along with the peas were cucumbers and tomatoes to be picked. These were sliced for noon and evening meals.

While the selected fresh vegetables were cooking, Minnie made cornbread, the one single staple item available three meals per day daily, either freshly baked or left over. This combination of meats, breads, and vegetables is just one example with the variety of combinations being almost endless.

When any of the dishes were cooked, the amount was usually enough to last several meals. So, any given meal, even breakfast, could be put together beginning with several dishes left over from other meals. One of the responsibilities of Minnie, the head of the kitchen, was to be aware at all times of the leftover dishes and whether the length of time since they were last heated to preserve them meant that they had to be heated in the current meal preparation cycle. In this manner, no food was wasted and the health of all who ate at the homestead table was preserved.

Other members of the family were regularly involved in the gathering of the home produce for preparation in the kitchen and home consumption. Often, school-age children did the picking of vegetables from the garden.

Some typical assignments in food gathering that were often given to children were picking of peas and beans, grappling of potatoes, and harvesting okra, tomatoes, cucumbers, squash, pumpkins, cushaws, or mirlitons (which we called alligator pears). We were often called upon to pull turnips, beets, carrots, onions, shallots, and radishes from the ground. We cut cabbage and picked leaves from the collard green stalks.

We often grappled potatoes with a grappling iron made from a piece of an old automobile spring leaf or a buggy spring leaf. It was just a one—to two-foot long piece of flat iron about two inches wide that was an excellent tool inserted under the mound of soil near the base of a potato plant and prize out the potato underneath, break it off the parent plant, and accumulate enough in this manner to make a dish. This procedure was used before the potato plants and crop matured and were dug. This procedure worked equally well on Irish potatoes or sweet potatoes.

One particular vegetable harvesting chore is most memorable to all who ever engaged in it. John D and Minnie had seed which they saved from season to season and from crop to crop on most crops grown on the homestead. One of these treasured seeds was that of "cow horn" okra. I have seen the stalks of cow horn okra grow sixteen feet tall. The pods of cow horn okra could grow to be twelve inches in length and still be a tender fresh vegetable dish for a meal.

The memorable thing about being sent to pick the okra was that this variety, as most varieties of okra had at that time, had a fierce velvety fuzz growing on each stalk and pod of okra, and letting it touch your skin was enough to set your arms to itching for an hour. I have seen my mother take a pair of sleeves off an old, discarded, man's work shirt and fashion mittens that covered her arms up to her elbows to pick okra.

Later in the 1930s, I remember Minnie acquiring some seed for a variety of okra called velvet okra, which was supposed to be itch free. For the most part it was.

However, it did not produce half as much okra as the old cow horn variety.

Around 2009, Ruth told me she still has seed to Minnie's cow horn okra.

When fruit was ripe, we would in season pick apples, plums, pears, grapes, strawberries, and figs in addition to the vegetables. In the summer, both adults and children picked wild fruit. Many times, we canned numerous gallons of blackberries from the wild plants. In less volume, we preserved gallons of huckleberries, sometimes called blueberries. Sometimes we harvested enough wild grapes to can several gallons of grape juice.

Occasionally we found enough mayhaws to make mayhaw jelly. Much jelly and jam was made from several fruits, particularly blackberries, plums, mayhaws, grapes, and huckleberries.

Canning of all the fruits and vegetable was a rather simple and straightforward process. We saved our fruit jars from year to year so we only had to buy a few new ones each year. We simply purchased the little flat discs for the lids which had a glued-on rubber gasket to make it seal. That is the configuration in which they can be purchased to this day in the local supermarkets.

We processed the fruit and seasoned with salt, sugar, and/or spice for canning. When it was ready to put in the jars, we washed and scalded the jars. Then we used a funnel and dipper or large spoon to ladle the fruit or vegetable into the jars. Next, we placed the two-part lid on the jar and left it loosely held on top of the jar. Several jars like this were placed into a large boiler with a top covering them. About two inches of water were added to the pot. A dishtowel was placed in the pot to keep the glass jars from being in contact with the metal pot, which could transmit so much heat in a small spot that the glass jar could crack. The cloth prevents this from happening. The loosely capped jars filled with cooked fruit or vegetables were steamed for about twenty minutes to assure that all microbes were killed. Then the boiler was removed from the top of the wood stove. Each jar was quickly removed from the boiler and the lid was tightened by hand. Dry cloths were used to grip the jar and lid to keep them from burning the hands. The jars were set aside for cooling. As the tiny bit of airspace left in each jar cooled, it shrunk and vacuum-sealed the lid to the top of the jar. It was entertaining, and still is, to seal the jars in this manner and listen for them to pop when the vacuum seal takes place.

A jar processed in this manner will preserve the contents for years.

One word of caution is appropriate, as we had to be sure to store the glass jars in a place in which the temperature did not go below freezing, thirty-two degrees Fahrenheit, as the contents of the jars would freeze, expand, and crack the glass.

We had a pantry of shelves located in our dining room, which was adjacent to the kitchen. The shelves had space enough to keep many gallons of food in jars from a half-pint to a gallon in size. When a heavy freeze was forecast, we kept fire burning in the kitchen stove all night to keep the jars from freezing and cracking.

On occasion, with so many jars on shelves, a jar would spoil. When it did, the jar cracked and the contents ran out. I remember this happening only a few times over about dozen years of assisting with the canning process. Some child in the learning process probably did not wash a jar well for reuse. Hence, a culprit microbe grew in the contents of the jar and spoiled the food.

I can remember helping can five gallons of peaches in a single afternoon. That is a lot of peaches to peal in one day. Several family members helped on that occasion. There were many days of canning such as this each year.

Later, during the winter, we would open a gallon container. Sometimes we would take a portion of the fruit and reprocess it and place it in smaller jars. I remember that, on one occasion, about half of a jar of peaches was separated and placed in a pot where they were converted by adding more sugar and cooking until peach jam was the resulting product. Homemade peach jam with homemade biscuits and butter is what we called eating "high on the hog." It was what we called, "Stomped down good."

Sometimes we canned tomatoes in one-gallon fruit jars. When a gallon of tomatoes was opened, we knew we were in for a treat. Minnie could take some meat from a freshly killed young goat, called "kid meat," cut it into hunks, add it to a pot of water, and cook it. She added tomatoes, cut up some potatoes, some carrots, and onions, and added them to the pot to make the most delicious homemade soup in the county.

This was served, virtually, as a one-dish meal with freshly cooked cornbread. Ever present to go with this was the milk, cream, butter, and cane syrup. Usually several other dishes were put on the table with the soup so plenty of variety was the norm.

I remember coming home late. Supper was already cold as I put my mule in the barn and fed her. I found the cold soup and cold cornbread, heated a saucepan of the soup on the stove, and ate the cornbread cold to help keep the hot soup from burning me. What a dish! I finished the meal with a bowl of cold milk with cornbread crumbled in it and some cane syrup poured over it for dessert.

Still eating high on the hog!

Meal preparation would not be complete without explaining that leftover food was kept in a "safe." A safe was an open cabinet screened to keep flies out, with shelves on which to place the dishes and bowls of food.

Not all food required being placed in the safe. For example, the center of the dining table was adorned with saltshaker, black pepper shaker, and sugar bowl with a cover on it. And any dish that was completely covered could also be left on the table until time to prepare the next meal.

We had screens on door and window openings to the kitchen and dining room. These screens kept out all but a few sneaky flies that would come in when someone opened a screen door to go in or out. To take care of those few flies was a fine job for a growing boy or girl. Get the fly swatter, kill the intruding pest, and clean up the area where the fly was killed. If the season was particularly bad for flies, we kept the hand-pumped spray gun filled with insecticide so we could saturate the atmosphere in an entire room in a few seconds, killing all flies contained therein. All containers of food had to be covered if this was done in kitchen or dining room. A clean—up period was required after such a treatment.

The leading brand of insecticide at the time was called Flit. Hence, just as it became the norm to refer to a soft drink as a Coke, it became the norm to refer to any liquid spray insecticide as Flit. It could be purchased in a can at any general merchandise store. That is the only kind of stores that existed in small towns in the piney woods of the South.

The county seat, or the parish seat of government in Louisiana, which had parishes instead of counties, was the nearest town to be large enough to have other than a general merchandise store.

Natchitoches, the largest city in Natchitoches Parish in the 1930s, had a population of 5,712, which, if I recall correctly, was announced on the welcome signs on highways entering the city at the city limits. This "huge metropolitan" area boasted an F. W. Woolworth department store and a Piggly Wiggly grocery store. The most noteworthy thing I remember about the Woolworth store was that it had central air-conditioning. That was the first building I ever entered that had central air-conditioning.

Neither The Nakatosh Hotel on Main Street nor Hughes Men's Clothing Store, also on Main Street, was air conditioned. Natchitoches did offer some other amenities. Ice cream could be bought a block off Main Street at a place named Lay's Best Yet Icecream.

A couple of drugstores were in business. In the 1930s, Harry Hawthorne owned the largest general merchandise store in Provencal, Louisiana. From time to time, over the years, there were one, two, or three others which opened for short periods of years.

Such a spray as Flit was often used to relieve livestock which were under stress because of flying insects like mosquitoes and horseflies.

To this day, I cannot open a refrigerator without giving thanks for being able to afford electricity and refrigeration, which made the old "safe" obsolete.

CHAPTER 21

# Building a Mud Chimney

It was about 1930 when a log cabin was built on the Sylvest homestead to become the residence of Vince Sylvest, eldest son of John D and Minnie Sylvest.

I remember only the work I observed done by John D plus his three oldest sons, Vince, Frank, and Spurgeon, as I was only five years old at the time. After eighty years, the author's memory may be a bit fuzzy.

The two-story, single-pen log cabin with a partitioned kitchen area was built and the roof put on. Then an opening was cut in the logs at the bottom of the north wall of the area that was to become the living room. The opening looked to me like a short door. It was about five feet wide by five feet tall. The floor was thirty inches from the ground. Four heart pine posts were placed in postholes dug for the purpose and slats of wood were nailed to make a small pen at the base of the posts. An area of floor was cut out which was to become the hearth of the fireplace. Below the hearthstones, hematite from a gravel quarry about two miles away was piled in a box that had been constructed in place for that purpose. On top of these stones, clay was packed and tamped. Then two layers of earth and two layers of brick were laid at floor level.

The slats, about one inch by two inches, which were nailed on one row at a time from the ground up on the chimney posts had a bit of Spanish moss draped over them. Clay was dug from a pit in our pasture about a hundred yards from the chimney and hauled on a slide to the site. Near the chimney, another pit about three feet wide was dug in which to mix the clay. Selected clay was put into the pit and water from the creek about a hundred yards away was poured in the pit to mix the clay and water to a consistency that would make a ball about five inches in diameter which could be handled by one man in his two hands. Spanish moss was mixed into each ball of clay. The bottom slat nailed to the rectangular base of the chimney was covered by a layer of mud and moss, which resulted in a mud wall on the chimney about six inches thick. The same was done on each of the four sides of the chimney except in the opening in the room which was to become the fireplace. When one row of slats was covered with the mud moss mixture, another row of slats was nailed on top of the growing wall of the chimney to the posts on all four sides. Thus, the four walls of the chimney went up the side of the two-story building to about two feet above the roof.

This was such an extraordinary event that it was planned weeks in advance and neighbors from miles around were invited. I have no memory of the number of people who were present. However, I remember there was a crowd of men. The speed with which that chimney went up was unbelievable. Men were hauling mud from the pasture. Men were mixing the balls of mud with Spanish moss. When the man making the balls completed one, he gave it to another man who tossed the ball, known as a "mud cat," up to a man who placed it on the next slat, row after row.

I was not allowed to stick around to observe the whole process as I walked the quarter of a mile back to our house with my mother, begging to be allowed to stay with my dad the whole way.

Not to be for this complaining five-year-old.

When I next saw the chimney, about a week later, it looked like it had been there for a long time and was just the normal chimney on a house. John D had again exhibited his multitude of talents in constructing another pioneer log cabin not unlike the one built by Nehemiah Sylvest, John D's father, in 1881 when John D was only two years old.

The 1881 structure is on the National Historic Register and is on exhibit in 2010 in the Mile Branch Settlement on the fairgrounds in Franklinton, Louisiana, in Washington Parish.

Vince's log cabin built in 1930 and 1931 burned to the ground from a fire set by an arsonist about 1950.

The affair of constructing the mud chimney was termed a "chimney raising." It was considered highly desirable to begin the job and continue uninterrupted except at night until it was complete. In that manner, the curing process that took place by maintaining a fire in the fireplace for several days around the clock to help harden the walls of the chimney made by the posts, slats, and mud cats could proceed without interruption and result in the chimney becoming monolithic in form and durability. One reason for this hurry was to avoid rain interfering with the wall building.

After the mud cats were draped over the slats all the way to the top the exterior surface and the top of the chimney was plastered with a mixture of the mud and something like lime to provide a protective covering resistant to the erosion from the beating it took over the years from rain and wind.

Around 1940, I had occasion to learn the steps in the above process when John D had occasion to repair one of the mud chimneys on our old home near Provencal, Louisiana, where I was born. However, much like my experience with the skills of goat management, I have never found much market for the skills of building mud chimneys.

# CHAPTER 22
# The Blacksmith Shop

Most of the families who lived in the piney woods of the South during the Great Depression did not own a blacksmith shop.

John D Sylvest owned a blacksmith shop, which he acquired when I was about ten years old in 1935.

Many hours did I stand by the forge, turning the handle to supply an even, controlled flow of air to the bed of coals my father was using to heat some piece of iron to fashion a needed part or tool. The handle did not need to be turned all of the time, but the young assistant to the blacksmith dared not be unavailable on a moment's notice to add charcoal to the fire or turn the blower at just the speed demanded by the smithy. This was a fertile learning environment for a high school age student.

The largest job of ironwork I remember was the making of new steel axles for a homemade wagon fashioned from an old horse-drawn road grader. John D had acquired the wagon from Harvey Crittendon of Provencal. The axles were well worn when he traded something for the wagon. We had some steel shafts about two and a half inches in diameter that had come from an abandoned sawmill site on our homestead quarter section of piney woods.

I assure you that cutting that shaft the right length by heating it in the fire and cutting it into two pieces when red hot by placing the red section on the anvil and cutting with a chisel held by a pair of steel tongs was not a job for a kid. John D had the knowledge, strength, and experience. He and I worked many hours on that piece of shaft, tapering the ends so they would receive the hubs of the steel grader wheels. After the ends were tapered, a hole had to be punched into the end of the axle so a steel pin could be inserted to hold the wheel on the axle.

For a four-wheeled wagon, four such shaft ends were required by the necessary two axles. That job required what seemed to me to be almost an entire summer. I recall being some relieved that the axles had been completed and had been installed on the wagon. Just maybe I would recover some of my playtime, which had been sorely reduced during my seeming exile to the blacksmith shop.

A second job I remember was the rebuilding of a wooden wagon wheel which was fitted with a steel rim. I delighted in watching John D take the old wheel apart by removing the steel rim and setting it aside. He then removed the pieces of felloes, the outer portions of the wheel to which the spokes were attached. Not all of the felloes required replacement. Tools used in this operation were hand tools. I recall that he kept the arc of the felloes the same as the discarded pieces by using the old felloes as a pattern, to lay out the design on the new piece of wood from which new felloes were to be fashioned. After he made them, he then checked the arc by placing them against the good parts left on the wheel.

The cutting of that wood was something to observe. John D used a handsaw and an axe to rough cut the piece of wood. I do not recall the tree from which the wood was cut, probably oak. After rough cutting, he worked more wood off with an adze, a wood-cutting tool made like a hoe. Then he did the fine finishing work with a drawknife. With a brace and bit, he bored the holes into the felloes into which the spokes were to be inserted. Finally, he used a wood rasp to file away the last traces of extra wood. The end product looked just as finished as the originals on the undamaged wheels. I was amazed.

After installing the new spokes in the hub and inserting them into the holes drilled in the felloes, John D positioned the wheel hub on the ground with supports under the spokes and felloes.

Separately, he mounted the rim on several pieces of iron so the rim was held about six inches from the ground. He piled pine knots all along the entire circumference of the wheel and lit all of them at one time so they would burn simultaneously. John D handed me a pair of tongs and said to me, "Son, when I tell you, you put those tongs right here on this rim and I am going to get on the other side. While it is still hot, we are going to lift it and slide it down over the wheel." After the rim was well heated but somewhat below the temperature where it turned red hot, John D said, "Now, son!" Whereupon he kicked all the fire away from the rim and grabbed his side of the rim with his tongs, directing me to hurry and grab the rim across from him. We struggled with the heavy rim but finally got it over the wheel. He grabbed his blacksmith shop hammer and hammered the rim down over the wooden wheel. As the rim contacted, the wood of the wheel smoked from the heat of the hot rim. As that steel rim shrunk, I could see the wood compressed into the tighter configuration. The rim was so hot when we placed it on the wood that the wood started smoking. However, John D, knowing that would be the case, was prepared with the water to cool and shrink the rim.

An admiring son, again, stood in awe of the skills of his dad.

Neighbors often came with old files used to sharpen hoes and saws around the farm for John D to use in making a butcher knife type knife for home use. I never had the available file to attempt to make a knife out of it, but some of those knives lasted for years. How he kept those files from breaking while he hammered an edge on them I can only imagine. As I looked on and turned the handle to keep the blower feeding oxygen to the flame, I could see the work piece as he held the file on the surface of the anvil and hammered the edge of the file with tiny strokes of a small hammer and soon returning the file to the forge to keep the temperature just right for his crafting of a new kitchen knife. Finally, as he regarded the fashioning step completed, he returned the new knife to the glowing coals for the final heating to just the right temperature for him to use in quenching the edge of the new blade and finally the whole blade of the knife, gradually, until it was cooled, tempering it so it would not be too hard to sharpen or too brittle and subject to breaking under normal kitchen use. We had several of these knives that John D had made that lasted until I was a grown man.

As a finishing touch, John D ground the edges of these knives on a foot-driven grinding wheel. The operator of the wheel sat on a seat similar to a bicycle seat and pedaled with one pedal lever made of wood to turn the crank mounted in the center of the grinding stone sharpening wheel. I spent many hours sharpening axes and hoes using that wheel. It was an effective tool to shine the entire side of a new knife blade as well as to sharpen the cutting edge. Occasionally a knife was made with two cutting edges like a dagger. Such a knife was handy for sticking a hog by cutting his aorta.

I was always ready to take on the demanding job of helper to the blacksmith because I was going to learn something new from the master, my dad.

One day I had been plowing in a field and one of the plows I was using had become horribly dull. I was about fourteen years old. That would have been about 1939. When I came to the house from the field at noontime, I told my dad, "Papa, that heel sweep on that plow is so dull it will hardly cut through the grass roots as I plow. I need you to sharpen it for me."

His reply was, "Sharpen it yourself; you know how to do it."

So, instead of heading straight for the field to resume my plowing after eating lunch, I proudly headed for the blacksmith shop, built a fire, heated the dull heel sweep, and began to hammer a sharp edge on the red-hot steel.

Any experienced blacksmith knows that when sharpening the edge of a straight piece of flat metal, the blade portion tends to form a circle as one edge is hammered to make it thinner, hence sharper. The kid working on this particular heel sweep did not realize, or had forgotten, that he must draw the metal out by hammering it on the opposite edge enough to compensate for that tendency and keep his work piece straight.

After working on that heel sweep for about an hour, it looked like a bird about to take flight. Each side had curled into a neat four-inch hook at the end of the heel sweep. It looked not unlike the fleur-de-lis of the Saints football team emblem.

When I showed it to John D and asked him what I was doing wrong, he must have been suffering because he wanted to laugh so bad. However, credit that man with one of the greatest compliments that a son could ever give to a father. John D did not laugh at my error. He never forgot to use every such occasion as a teaching experience for his children. He never forgot that one of his primary responsibilities to his children was to teach them so they would be able to take care themselves.

He and I went back to the blacksmith shop together and he demonstrated the drawing of hot iron on an anvil with a shop hammer to me.

I did not realize at the time, but he had been willing to sacrifice that worn-out old twenty-two-inch heel sweep for me to learn how to sharpen a plow in the blacksmith shop. I do believe he knew all along that after I hammered on that heel sweep for a while it would never be useful as a plow again. He probably had decided that it was ready to throw away anyway.

After the blacksmith shop lesson, he handed me a new sixteen-inch heel sweep and said, "Here, son, use this one."

Sometimes the job in the blacksmith shop was for a neighbor or a friend. That afforded me the opportunity to visit with the sons of our neighbors, all of whom were friends.

One of the most useful devices in the blacksmith shop was the steel vise. In it, a work piece, either metal or wood, could be clamped tightly so it could be worked on with a tool. This step was commonly used to hold a piece of iron which had to be cut with a hacksaw. No power saws were available. Just cut it by hand with a handsaw if cutting wood, or with a hacksaw if cutting metal.

The vise came in handy to hold a work piece through which a hole had to be bored with a brace and bit. No power drills were available either. Just put pressure on the top of the brace with your chest and turn the crank with the strength of your arms to bore a hole in a piece of wood.

I still possess the brace which I bought new in 1946 after World War II. I used it a few years until I could become the proud owner of an electricity-powered drill motor and live in a place that had electricity.

John D was not a joke teller, as he regarded it as a waste of time and hence not following the straight and narrow. However, he let his guard down once in a while. On one occasion, he told of the blacksmith who was doing some preliminary work on some horseshoes. As he heated and hammered each horseshoe one at a time, he dipped it into a tub of water then tossed it on top of a tub filled with sand where it could continue to cool. The blacksmith had just pitched a hot shoe on to the tub of sand when a stranger walked up.

The stranger reached down and picked up that nearly red-hot horseshoe, quickly dropping the shoe back on the sand, whereupon the blacksmith, laughing, asked, "What's the matter? Is that horseshoe hot?"

The stranger said, "Nope, it just don't take me long to inspect a horseshoe."

Royce, my younger brother, and I thought the joke was twice as funny because our dad had loosened up enough to tell a good joke.

The anvil from John D's blacksmith shop, which burned to the ground when I was overseas in World War II, is now preserved in the Jefferson Parish Historical Society's museum blacksmith shop in Gretna, Louisiana. It is used as a bell to strike when a couple chooses to be married in a historic blacksmith shop wedding. When struck with a steel hammer, it produces a grand ringing sound, pleasant and audible to ears fifty feet away.

Not all anvils produce a clear, loud ring when struck by the steel hammer. For this reason, the Jefferson Parish Historical Society had been searching for some time for a ringing anvil when I learned of their search and presented them with John D's old anvil.

I am happy to report here that the practice of the trade of blacksmithing is still preserved in the Sylvest family tree by Glen Wesley, husband of Barbara Sylvest Wesley of Baton Rouge, Louisiana. His skills are still sought out by clients all over the United States here in the twenty-first century.

Yes, siree! Blacksmithing was an integral part of our survival when I was growing up in the piney woods near Provencal during the Great Depression.

# CHAPTER 23
# All Day Singing and Dinner on the Ground

All Day Singing and Dinner on the Ground was truly a Southern tradition of the years of the Great Depression in the rural South. It was in 1929 when I had just made four years old that my mother's health had deteriorated to the point at which she could no longer endure the five-mile ride in a mule-drawn wagon to church each Sunday.

It was at that time that John D, my father, decided to build a church on Sylvest Road in Natchitoches Parish five miles south of Provencal. This process took about two years. That log cabin church was named Mt. Nebo Baptist Church.

In the meantime, Harmony Baptist Church was just four miles through the woods from our home. Occasionally we went there.

During the 1930s, there was a Baptist Church about every five miles throughout the settled rural areas of north Louisiana. This spacing met the needs of the time for memberships which traveled to church on Sundays by walking, riding horseback, or riding in a mule-drawn wagon. The latter was our family style, if you are willing to let me use the word *style* with a few degrees of freedom.

Roughly the same pattern applies to the distribution of Methodist, Assembly of God, and other Protestant denominations as well.

Harmony Baptist Church could not afford a full-time pastor. So, the minister, whom the congregation designated as its pastor, came and preached only on one chosen Sunday of the month, such as the second Sunday. Services were conducted on other weekends by laymen from the congregation plus an occasional visiting minister.

Since this pattern prevailed at most of the local churches, this left the fifth Sunday of each month with five Sundays open with no ordained minister engaged to conduct church services. This was seized upon by the musically inclined portion of the membership as a time for a weekend of singing and potluck type eating, which was designated as an "All Day Singing and Dinner on the Ground" service.

For example, the year 2010 has only four months with five Sundays: January, May, August, and October. Scheduling this function on the fifth Sunday assured that the other four Sundays when the pastor would be needed to preach were not interfered with.

The church chosen for this function was alternated among the locations so people for miles around got the opportunity to have their turn at hosting the affair.

Harmony Baptist Church, about three miles from Provencal and three miles from Flora, was one of the favorite spots. I have always thought the presence of an outstanding family of singers named Roberts was probably responsible for that popularity of the Harmony location. Several of the family were ordained ministers and several more were accomplished song leaders and musicians and lived nearby.

One renowned member of that family was Reverend Monroe Roberts of Bellwood, Louisiana. Brother Monroe's Model A Ford was known and recognized all over Natchitoches Parish as Reverend Roberts drove from church to church to serve his congregations. I remember that Oscar and Oliver Roberts, two of his brothers, were also ministers and accomplished song leaders. As I recall, Oscar Roberts also played the piano.

Some other outstanding citizens named Roberts who were brothers or cousins and who lived in the vicinity were Gay, Jimmie, William, and Steve. All of the above were friends or our family.

All of the above often attended the singings.

When the time arrived for the singing, some preparations were made. Announcements were sent to surrounding churches informing the countryside of the affair. Gospel quartets and singing groups like the Stamps Quartet from Arkansas were invited. Sometimes whole families of singers were invited as special guests. The renowned Carter family of radio fame was typical of some of the singing families who came, although I do not remember the Carter family being at Harmony.

Not on your life do you think the church elders were going to let an opportunity for someone to preach go by the wayside. So, one of the ministers who did not have to go to serve another congregation, as a duty, was engaged to preach at each service at the singing, morning and evening. A special collection was taken at each service for the respective preacher who spoke.

During my elementary school years, I was blessed to be able to attend these local events when an older sibling would allow me to go along.

I loved the singing and still do. I remember many of the old traditional gospel songs by heart. Many of the songs I have heard hundreds of times during my lifetime.

As a ten-year-old in the fourth grade, I remember going to Harmony one Sunday. When we arrived, having driven a wagon four miles across the woods on an unimproved road, the first thing I looked for was the water barrel. Remember: no electricity, no running water. Some of the deacons of the church had accepted the responsibility of providing cool water for the whole congregation. The container was a fifty-five-gallon oaken barrel obtained from The Coca-Cola Bottling Company in Natchitoches. It had been a container of Coca-Cola syrup. Some church member had made a special trip to Natchitoches with a pickup truck and purchased a hundred-pound block of ice. There were few pickup trucks. I am almost certain that the only person at Harmony with a truck at the time was William Roberts. When the ice arrived at Harmony Church, it was broken in half and one-half was put in the barrel. The barrel had been filled with water by taking the barrel to a spring about a mile from the church. The remaining half of the ice was carefully wrapped back in the burlap wrapping so it would not melt. An eleven-year-old would notice such things, especially if it was the first ice water he had ever had.

Not to be minimized was the time to eat. The singing went on all morning, interrupted only by the sermon, which began at about 11:00 a.m. and ended about noon.

When time to eat was declared, all the mothers scrambled for their baskets and spread their food in a community arrangement on tables built for that purpose on the church grounds.

I knew that our basket had only cornbread and biscuits in it. I also knew that some of the other baskets contained "light" bread. We regarded light bread as a rare treat at our home. Sure enough, one of James Kay's sisters had made some peanut butter and jelly sandwiches and I got two of them. Little country boy gone to heaven is what I thought I was. In a few minutes, I was thirsty and went to get cup after cup of that cold ice water from the barrel. The water was available in little cone-shaped paper cups.

Other dishes that were popular were chicken and dumplings, fried chicken, and cakes and pies made with blackberries, plums, pears, apples, and peaches.

The meal was truly a feast as each lady who brought food cooked her favorite recipe for the occasion. We ate well, though we were regarded as being "as poor as Job's turkey." I was playing with Raymond Kay, who had come with his family across the same unimproved road to get to the church. I was some impressed with the Kay wagon. It was the only wagon on the church grounds which was new and was still covered with the original green and red paint. It was only recently, about seventy years after the event, that I was informed by James Kay that his older brother, Rufus, who had gone to work in the oil fields, had purchased that wagon for his father, P. G. Kay.

Raymond and I took advantage of the noon break to ramble about the grounds and investigate such things as hitching rails to which saddle horses were tied. Off to the side about fifty feet was a block of wood which was used as a mounting block by ladies who had difficulty getting on a horse. I have often wondered what ever happened to that mounting block. What an appealing antique.

It was only a couple of years before Raymond got a broken arm when the team pulling their wagon spooked on the gravel road. The accident occurred close to the Longinos' place near Horsepen Creek and the wagon turned over. The team was made up of a horse named Charlie and a mule named Rube. Rube was skittish of vehicles. When a CCC truck whizzed by the wagon and left a huge cloud of dust, Rube spooked. He ran off the road and down a steep bank, turning the wagon over. I felt sorry for my friend when he had to wear a cast to school.

It was late one evening when we were nearing the end of the service and nearly all the congregation had already gone home from one of these Singings. One of the deacons got up and passed his hat to take a collection for the preacher. The whole amount collected was only about two dollars. The deacon passed the hat again saying, "We can't let the preacher go away with only two dollars." The deacon passed the hat again and got less than another dollar, so he decided to pass the hat the third time, appealing to those present to dig deeply and give generously. When the hat got to Mr. William Roberts, Mr. Roberts said, "Thee will give the durn mess ten dollars." Whereupon he put a ten-dollar bill into the hat.

I doubt if there was another man in the church who had as much as ten dollars in his pocket.

To this day, I recall fondly the All Day Singings and Dinners on the Ground during the Great Depression.

## CHAPTER 24

# Dipping Cattle in Louisiana during the 1930s

Sylvest farm near Provencal had a visitor from the Louisiana Department of Agriculture during my ninth year, 1934. That was the year I lost my new penny which my brother-in-law, Walter "Son" Moss had given me for my birthday. Who could forget a thing like that?

Our visitor was my uncle, Harrison Fendlason, brother to my mother, whose maiden name was Minnie Ora Fendlason.

Uncle Harrison was in the vicinity of Provencal on an official mission of the Louisiana Department of Agriculture, his employer, as he was traveling over the state to publicize the program of Texas Cattle Fever Tick eradication, which was forthcoming in the state.

I remember his setting up a projector in our living room and showing a movie film of the process of dipping cattle in a solution of what we called "creosote dip."

I cannot remember what the source of energy was to operate the projector, but I seem to remember a gasoline engine running while we watched the brief film. I distinctly remember seeing the cattle in the film jumping into the dipping vats and swimming to the other end, where they climbed up an inclined concrete ramp to a holding pen where they were allowed to drip dry briefly before they were allowed to return to large holding pens.

Within a few weeks, some men were digging and cementing the walls and bottom of a dipping vat nine-tenths of a mile from our homestead. It was located on the northwest corner of the intersection of what is now Sylvest Road and LA Highway 117, about five miles south of Provencal.

I believe it was 1935 when the eradication program required the dipping of all cattle, horses, mules, and donkeys. All our neighbors had cattle on the open range, as did my father. Each owner knew his cattle. Some owners branded their cattle. Not all my father's cattle were branded, but those that were wore an "S" on their left shoulder. That brand was registered in the name of John D Sylvest at the Louisiana State Brands office.

Dipping all the cattle in the community was the single event that elicited more cooperation from the entire population of the community than any other I have experienced in my eighty-five years.

When the announcement was made that the cattle of our community were to be assembled and dipped on a certain date, everyone talked to their neighbors about how many cattle each one had, where those cattle were, who in the owner's family was capable of driving and being responsible for getting that particular herd to the dipping vat, and who was going to help whom.

A nine-year-old could do a lot of cattle driving, but to my dismay, I was not identified as "old enough" to be turned loose in the woods riding a mule to do the roundup.

During the week preceding the dipping, my older brothers had rounded up all the family herd and driven them into a pen where they were fed and watered until dipping day.

Someone coordinated the sequence in which the owners would drive their particular herd to the vat. Owners then gathered at the holding pen where animals were held after dipping until the owner's count was verified. Once the number of cattle was verified, that owner was permitted to drive his herd from the pen homeward.

The fences required to build these pens around the dipping vats were made of rough, sawed oak lumber. One-inch, rough-sawed, dry, oak boards are extremely hard wood.

In later years, I salvaged some of the boards for use on our farm. Other residents salvaged some also.

State inspectors attended each dipping session. More than one dipping session took place, though I do not recall how many. From reading of the program, I learned in later years that more than one dipping session was required in order to break the life cycle of the pests.

While the state of Louisiana was declared "fever tick free" in the 1940s, the remnants of the eradication program are still in effect in the United States, as they have been since 1906.

It is my wish to return to the site and search for the old concrete vat which was built there in 1934 or 1935.

# CHAPTER 25
# Quilting

Quilts were the primary covers used to keep warm in bed in the homes of the sand hills of the South before and during the Great Depression. Our bedrooms had no heat, no fireplaces, and no stoves.

Most quilts were handmade in the home of the owner. Many of the quilts in our home were made right there in what we called our "front room" or "living room." The room was the largest one in the house. A wood-burning fireplace was at one end of the room.

Scraps of all cloth materials that were not large enough to make a garment were saved at our house. That house was the destination of many a piece of US mail, which was a box of scraps sent by some relative or friend who knew my mother well enough to know that she could and would use every scrap suitable for making quilt tops. She and some of the other ladies, from our piney woods neighborhood, even sewed diaper shirts out of some of those scraps of material and sent them to foreign missionaries in Africa. We always had boxes and boxes of scraps.

There are so many ways to make a quilt top that they are still being invented.

One of the classic ways was for the seamstress in charge of the project to select a quilt top pattern. The pattern chosen would have a characteristic sub-part called "squares," which were of a predetermined dimension, typically about eighteen inches square.

One of the simplest designs, and one often used in the piney woods of the rural South, was just smaller squares, which would be stitched together until the larger square was constructed. One reason for this pattern choice is that it was simple for everyone to understand. One need not be a skilled seamstress or an accomplished quilt maker to make a big contribution to the total labor demand of making a quilt. This was even within the capacity of preteen children. I remember sitting around the fireplace and helping cut out the smaller squares of material, for example, four inches square from material of designated color or pattern design so the squares of the quilt top would all be identical.

That pattern might call for a red piece of material on each of the four corners of each square. Obviously, they could be of any geometric shape and size so long as, when properly stitched together, they formed the squares.

As I recall, when material was scarce and the talent and time available were limited, the rules of the quilting were relaxed in favor of speeding up the project and getting the job finished so those needing the cover could be availed of it sooner.

I recall that cutting out quilt scraps was fun and so was stitching them together. The same for the quilting. There really was little such work I ever got involved in, as the sheer amount of the outside work of the fields, pastures, woods, and animals was always demanding. That outside work was regarded as men's and boys' work, and the indoor work of sewing and meal preparation was regarded as ladies' and girls' work.

As soon as I got big enough to plow, about ten years old, there was no more quilt training for me.

The quilting frame used to hold the work piece was made on the homestead. It consisted of four pieces of wood. Each piece of wood measured about three-fourths of an inch thick, two and one-half inches wide, and eight feet long. Each of the four boards had holes bored in them about four inches apart. The holes were about five-eighths of an inch in diameter. These four pieces were not sawed on a mill but were split out of a tree with hand tools.

When four boards of the frame were assembled, wood pegs were shoved into the holes of two pieces of frame to keep the frame rigid and the quilt taut.

A quilt to be used on a standard double bed measured about six feet wide by seven feet long.

The process of fitting the materials to the frame preparatory to sewing were as follows.

Lining material was selected and procured—the determining factor in the selection was usually whatever was available. If one could afford the price, a quilt lining of chosen material and color could be ordered by US mail from Sears and Roebuck mail order catalog. Few homes were without such a catalog. Quilt linings were wider than the bolts of standard cloth.

Sometimes the linings were made of other material, such as the sacks in which foodstuffs and feedstuffs were purchased. Flour sacks were often used.

When the lining was selected and trimmed to size, it was attached along one edge to one of the four wooden frames by basting, sewing it with a long whipstitch to the frame.

Next, the opposite edge of the lining was stitched in the same way to another frame.

On this lining was placed the batting, which was loose cotton lint which had been milled for that purpose. It came in a roll and was easy to spread in an even thickness over the whole quilt lining.

If the batting was not available or could not be bought because of shortage of money, a perennial problem of the time, other cloth could be used to thicken the quilt.

The quilt top was placed on top of the batting and the three layers of the quilt were basted in place. That is, they were loosely sewn together so they would not change position until after the stitching of the quilting was completed.

There were four hooks screwed into the ceiling of the room to which the four heavy strings to hold the quilting frame up were attached. The strings hanging from the ceiling were simply wound around the wood frames and tied. That gave the quilters the flexibility of adjusting the quilt height from the floor to fit their size and chair height. At the end of the session of quilting, the frame could be pulled up by the strings so house occupants could walk under it or the space could be used for other living activities.

Picture two pieces of frame with quilt lining attached to them fastened to the four ceiling hooks. The other two pieces of frame were then placed across the ends of the ones hanging, making a rectangular frame. Holes were matched so the pegs could be placed through both wood frames, keeping the quilt material taut enough to make the stitches with the quilting needles.

Quilts were made of three layers of material: the lining, the batting, and the top. The top was the decorative side of the quilt and usually finished in a pre-chosen pattern, many of which were traditional. Otherwise, scraps of material were cut and stitched together into quilt squares which were then stitched together to make the entire quilt top. The patterns and designs for the quilt tops is unlimited, as each is a work of art.

The assembled lining, batting and top were wound around the two wood frames along the sides of the quilt, as the sides is where all the quilting is done. The first turns of quilting were laid out by the quilt owner or homeowner, or the quilter deemed the most expert at the occupation, often the same person.

Thread and needles, usually furnished by the hostess, were available to quilters when they were ready to begin. Most frequently, the word was passed around the community days before, as planned, so the hostess knew how many quilters were coming and who they were. Sometimes the hostess would prepare a meal a day in advance so she could join in the quilting.

Each quilter would lay out an area approximately eighteen inches across in whatever pattern had been prescribed for the particular quilt and stitch around the perimeter with the first row of stitches. Sometimes these patterns were marked and sometimes the experienced quilters just went to town knowing exactly what they were doing from years of practice. Time was taken to train beginners and younger quilters.

I learned to quilt when I was about thirteen years old. I was a fieldworker at that age and out with the men in the fields during the day. However, my mother taught all her sons as well as daughters to quilt. Her reason was, "Because you never know what you will be called upon to do in your life and you will be better off if you learn how to do more things."

It took strong hands and fingers to push the needle and pull the thread through the layers of the quilting material. A thimble was provided for this purpose. Most seamstresses had their favorite thimble. I remember my mother's favorite thimble well. It was worn enough that the brass under the outer shiny chrome coating showed through.

One reason I remember that thimble so well is that when the youngest three—Ruth, Royce, and I—were playing around the quilters, if we got into a spat and needed a bit of parental direction, the encouragement to obedience sometimes came by way of a thump on the head with that thimble. No, not child abuse, just more of that good old Southern character building.

After the first row of about eighteen inches was quilted on each side, that eighteen inches was rolled on to the piece of frame to which it had been attached by basting with long, loose stitches. This exposed the rest of the quilt to the reach of the quilters. This process continued until all of the quilt had been stitched. Then the edges were trimmed with scissors and the edges were folded into an even edge for hemming.

This completed the quilt. The entire process would sometimes be done by household members only. Other times, neighbors would assemble to help. If four ladies who were good quilters worked all day, they could finish a whole quilt.

This is an oversimplified explanation of the quilting process. Actually, it is a long-established fine art, and hundreds of books have been written on the subject.

This is just a memoir of a boy whose mother required him to learn to quilt when he was growing up on a sand hill farm during the Great Depression.

I never did learn to handle that thimble worth a darn.

# CHAPTER 26
# Sewing

Sewing was an integral part of subsistence living in the piney woods of Louisiana and the South during the Great Depression. My mother, Minnie, was an accomplished artist at the driver's seat of her Minnesota treadle (*treadle* means foot powered) sewing machine.

My five sisters learned to make their own dresses as soon as they were old enough. I recall that my younger sister, Ruth, could make a dress for herself using the Minnesota sewing machine by the time she reached high school at age thirteen.

Mrs. Minnie and that machine made an unforgettable pair. I can see my mother reaching for the flywheel on the sewing machine right now with her right hand to stop the machine suddenly to attend to numerous urgent tasks which interrupt a busy sewing mother: a pot boiling over on the stove nearby, a child screaming in the yard a few steps away as ants are stinging his feet, etc. Not stopping the machine properly could result in a tangle of wasted thread, which you can imagine. Because of her practiced touch, I seldom saw my mother with tangled thread.

Minnie Ora Fendlason Sylvest was a talented lady. She could cut a pattern from newspaper simply by holding the paper up against the future owner of the dress or shirt and looking at it and putting a few straight pins in it and trimming it with her scissors while she held it with the other hand, just like a professional tailor. If you had the job of clothing thirteen children, you were provided with the opportunity to learn many useful lessons. "Provided the opportunity," I say, as I often wondered if the root word of *provided* was the same as the root word for Providence. Dixie Sylvest Moss, my oldest sister who died in 2008 at age 102, told me when she was in her nineties about our mother teaching her to cut out patterns for clothing in the manner described. She used the skill to clothe herself and members of her family.

Being the daughter of a mother who owned and operated a spinning wheel did not impede Minnie's learning ability. Lillian Stringfield Fendlason, my grandmother, could sew a stitch or two herself, or spin, or knit, as the occasion demanded, aside from being able to play the piano, accordion, or organ, or teach music. If that will not improve your finger coordination, I don't know what would.

Minnie's nimble fingers and practiced eye produced most of the clothing worn by her growing brood, just as her mother's had done. Some of her alternate talents were manifested in her teaching piano lessons and playing piano and organ for churches.

I think I was eight years old before I wore a "ready-made" shirt. That's what we called a piece of clothing already manufactured when I was a kid growing up. Mrs. Lottie

Kay, one of our closest neighbors and mother of my good friend and classmate, James Kay, gave me a ready-made blue chambray shirt for my eighth birthday. Well, you could say that it was a big enough deal in my young life that I have never forgotten it. That's right, I am eighty-five years old, and it still is worth remembering and retelling. I loved that lady and I appreciated that shirt.

Other shirts I wore were homemade until I was almost grown. The same was true for my brothers' clothes as well as my sisters' dresses, gowns, and underwear.

As part of the apprenticeship which each child went through on that sand hill farm, sewing was one of the essential skills taught. Even the sons were taught the fundamentals of sewing with both the sewing machine and by hand. Minnie taught me to select the right thread size and color for the sewing task confronting me. Even the sewing on of a button, which has fallen off, requires some of such decisions. Basting two pieces of material together to hold them in place until they can be stitched on the machine requires the same decisions to be made. Again, the size of the needle on even the most basic sewing machine had to be matched to the weight of the material and the job the seam was designed to do. The same with respect to selection of the appropriate thread. Most thread was white as white thread was often used even on different colored material, such as in making quilts. While most quilt scraps were stitched together by hand, it was sometimes faster to smooth the material with a hot smoothing iron and stitch them together on the sewing machine.

I learned that buttonholes had to be bound by sewing almost microscopic stitches and material around them, because the constant buttoning and unbuttoning exposes the buttonhole to a lot of wear and tear.

The blind stitch is one stitch I remember. I used this stitch to sew stripes on my uniform during World War II. That was a skill which was much in demand. I was called on by friends so often for help in sewing stripes on that I began charging a dollar a stripe. That was a lot of money for me, someone who was only paid fifty-four dollars per month and from whose pay half was withheld by Uncle Sam and sent to a dependent parent.

Then there was the whipstitch and the saddle stitch. As you can see, I am not an accomplished seamstress or tailor. But the training and experience served me well when there was no knowledgeable skilled mom on whom to call.

Sewing by hand was the only way to get anything stitched when in a battle zone.

Uncle Sam provided a serviceman with a needle and about ten yards of thread, olive drab in color. I carried mine in my pocket inside my wallet the entire time I was overseas. I even continued the practice after the war was over as long as I was single.

John D Sylvest, my dad, had a supply of heavy-duty needles used for stitching heavy-duty materials and other specialized sewing jobs on the farm. One large, straight needle was used with heavy twine to assemble and repair white duck material used to make sacks to use in picking cotton. Another heavy-duty needle was kept with his shoe repair toolbox for use in repairing shoes of leather and other material. In most of the shoe repair stitching, the thread was waxed to make it waterproof.

A specially shaped bent needle called a speying needle was kept with the blacksmith shop tools which were used to suture wounds on hogs, cows, and goats. Special thread called "cat gut" to be used for suturing wounds on animals could be purchased. However, we used regular white, cotton, sewing thread dipped in pine tar as a substitute. After the suturing was completed, pine tar was poured over the wound, saturating it and effectively sealing the wound until it healed. I do not recall of a single instance in which the animal developed an infection in the wound. It was an effective method of managing wounds from castrating and speying as well as from accidents.

The speying needles were semi-flat and curved, making it easy to push the needle down through the edge of one side of a wound and back up through the edge on the other side. Surgeons still use curved needles for the same reason. Needles were also of different sizes, as different sized animals were involved.

I recall sitting by the fireside in the early winter and sewing a new strap to my cotton sack. I had gotten tired of having a piece of heavy twine looped over a green cotton boll compressed under a spot of material on the cotton sack.

That is still a good trick to know. If you wish to attach something contained inside a sack, you need not cut the sack. Simply slide a marble, cotton boll, or sweet gum ball inside the sack, gather material around it on the outside of the sack, then loop some twine over the material gathered around the object on the outside of the sack. You can tie anything to the twine without concern that it will come loose.

The large needles kept on the farm often came in handy for harness repair. It was easy to stitch several layers of burlap into a belt six inches wide to use as a back band to attach to trace chains on draft animals. One could envision this harness repair job as being infrequent and occasional. Not really so when the gear used, like ours, was so old and meager to begin with. Harness repair was a common fireside job of the evening during the Great Depression.

My mother's frequent admonishment to me, "Learn all you can, son, you never know when you will need to know it," echoes in my ears to this day, and my life experiences have proven her right.

# CHAPTER 27

# Getting a Spiritual Foundation: A Memoir

Keep in mind, as you read this memoir, that it begins in the 1920s when there were almost no improved roads and a sparse population of less than 130 million people in this old US of A. There were very few automobiles in the piney woods.

My father had two: a 1926 Model T Ford and about the same year Model T Ford truck. Neither of them was ever operated during my childhood. Most of the dozen or so other neighbors who lived within two miles of us had no automobile either. Only Ivey Honeycutt, who was a Star Route mail carrier, had one: a 1929 Model A Ford followed by later models beginning in 1937. If any members of my family, including my father, knew how to drive them, I am not aware of it. Never was it mentioned to me. They simply were left under the sheds where the tires, seat cushions, and canvas tops rotted off. John D and

Minnie Fendlason Sylvest had settled in on that quarter section of section 18 of piney woods on Sylvest Road in Natchitoches Parish five miles south of Provencal.

When they arrived there in 1923 to call it home, their choice of churches to attend was Bellwood Baptist Church five miles south of our home. There was no improved road in 1923. However, within five years, construction on Louisiana Highway 39, a gravel road from Leesville to Hagewood, Louisiana, was nearly completed.

When I first remember riding to Sunday school at Bellwood in a wagon, pulled by two mules, I was a preschooler not yet of the ripe old age of six years. The road we used was an improved gravel road for part of our route. I felt like the mules that pulled the wagon would have been happier if there had been no rocks to hurt their feet. I never rode to church in Bellwood, Louisiana, in an automobile.

My Sunday school teacher was named Mrs. Rhodes. I don't remember her husband's name, but they lived south and west of Bellwood Baptist Church.

Mrs. Rhodes had a large family of whom I remember Julian, a son about four years older than I, and Margie, a daughter about two years my senior.

There were several families who lived near Bellwood who invited our family to eat lunch with them after church services on Sunday. I recall visiting at the homes of Mr. Critt Murray; Rev. Monroe Roberts, the pastor; Gip Parker; Walter Moss Jr., my brother-in-law and Dixie's husband; and Mrs. Rhodes, my Sunday school teacher.

Sunday school classes began at 10:00 a.m. and lasted until about 11:00 a.m. One Sunday out of each month, we had a church service that lasted until 12:00 noon. That was the one Sunday out of four each month on which the pastor preached a sermon. I remember as a little child that the sermons seemed interminably long. They actually lasted less than an hour. To a three—or four-year-old, that is a long time to sit still.

The youngest children at home growing up during these 1920s, `30s, and `40s were Royce, born in 1930, Ruth, born in 1927, and me. I was born in 1925.

After I was born, my mother's health faltered and continued to keep her weak until after Ruth was born. This event I do not remember, so I rely on the story as told to me by my seven living older siblings: Dixie, Artie, Vince, Johnnie, Frankie, Spurgeon, and Pauline.

As Pauline was six years older than I, we three younger ones filled the home with babies and diapers again.

The combination of advancing age, a large family, a load of childcare to be performed, and hard times brought on by the Depression led our parents to stop trying to attend Sunday school and church services five miles from our home. Our wagon was badly worn and we had lost one of our three work animals, Nell, the mare that pulled our buggy. The buggy was worn out as well.

To offset these conditions, John D and Minnie enlisted several families who lived nearby and organized a new church parish. It was located on an acre of land donated by my parents on the corner of our farm near the road, which was only a hand-improved wagon trail. Some of the founding members of the new church, to become known as Mt. Nebo Baptist Church, were Jefferson and Jane Masters, John D and Minnie Sylvest, P. G. and Lottie Kay, and their immediate families.

The church building was built using pine trees donated and harvested from John D's and Minnie's farm. It was built by the church members and their children with volunteer labor from other neighbors. Trees were traded to the lumber mill in exchange for the cutting and hauling of timber and lumber. Then sawed lumber was bartered to the planing mill where much of the lumber was planed and milled on shares.

Some details of design and construction of this structure may be found elsewhere.

This provides a kind of a picture of the physical surroundings and the changes that were taking place in them during my formative years.

When we ceased going to Bellwood on Sundays, about 1929, my mother immediately began her own Sunday school classes for her three youngest children as we were born.

My first memories of that exercise was that on each Sunday morning on which the weather permitted, Minnie led Ruth and me over the hill in front of our house with her Bible and Sunday school lesson book. She selected three blackjack oak trees about three feet apart and situated in a triangle and said these three trees are going to be our church house until we get one built.

We are going to call these three trees the Father, the Son, and the Holy Spirit.

I recall each Sunday Minnie read our Sunday school lesson, which was a Scripture study and story supporting some part of the gospel message.

Each week Minnie assigned each of us a new Scripture verse to memorize. I recall her distinctly explaining to us that we had no guarantee that we would always carry the Bible with us wherever we would go in the world. In many parts of the world, the Bible was, and is, forbidden. Or we could be imprisoned and not have access to it. In the event of such developments in life, Minnie pointed out that it was important for us to have memorized important portions of the Bible so it could never be taken away from us.

In our home, we had a piano; my mother and five sisters played the piano. Two brothers played the piano as well. So we played and sang hymns from the church hymnals commonly used by several Protestant denominations at the time, such as Baptist, Methodist, Pentecostal, Assembly of God, Apostolic, Church of Christ, and Presbyterian, that I can recall, not to exclude others.

As a consequence of all this music around daily, I grew up memorizing the words and tunes to the songs I heard and learned to love them. Most of them were evangelical in nature. That is, they were composed with the idea that the listener could be induced to become a believer through listening to the words of the songs. It worked. My training was certainly reinforced by the repetitive messages contained in such songs as "Jesus Loves Me," "What a Friend," and "Amazing Grace."

By the time I could read, Minnie would have me stand up in the triangle of oak trees on the side of the hill in the piney woods and read our Sunday school lesson out loud. This was excellent grooming for taking leadership positions later on. As Ruth and Royce progressed to where they could read, they joined in and took their turns.

Each Sunday, we had to recite from memory the Scriptures we had been assigned to memorize that week. As the growing up years went by, the list of Scriptures I had committed grew to be quite lengthy. We were called upon to recite the sections that we had memorized earlier so we would not forget them. I recall that by the time our church house was built, I had already memorized the first five chapters of the gospel of Matthew, which is known as the Sermon on the Mount. Many other selections of Scripture I had memorized as well. I can still recite many of these passages from memory.

Other memory assignments included the Ten Commandments and the Lord's Prayer, which I learned later in life that Catholics referred to it as the "Our Father."

This seems to be a good spot for me to inform my readers, if any are unaware, that I was a Baptist until I was twenty-eight years old, at which time I became a Catholic. Don't worry about that too much, as it is not the major part of the story. God did not change.

In reflection, the Scriptures I memorized and the ones which we studied repeatedly when I was a child are largely the same ones which are considered most important by most mainline Christian denominations, Protestant or Catholic.

They remain the Scriptures I treasure.

# CHAPTER 28
# Caring for Animals

The daily routine of caring for animals was understood and shared by the whole household during the Great Depression on the Sylvest homestead. It is necessary to refer to "household" members rather than simply "family" members because the household frequently was composed of several individuals in addition to family members. Every one of them was sometimes involved in animal care.

A frequent command heard directed to a young child was, "Go open the gate and let the cows into the pasture." Another one was, "Go salt the goats and turn them loose."

Each day began with the determination of whether or not the harness or saddle work animals were to be used in the activities planned for the day. If the team of two mules was to be used, they were the first animals fed. This assignment went automatically to one of the older boys in the family.

Chores, including the care of the animals, were portioned out according to the age level of the house occupants and changed when the members of the household changed.

A sample day when I was a teenager and member of a household of two elderly parents, one grown older brother, a teenage sister, and a preteen younger brother would go as follows.

Before daybreak, around 4:00 a.m., Frank, the grown brother, went to the barnyard and fed the mules. He returned to the house where he prepared breakfast.

While Frank was cooking breakfast, biscuits, and bacon to go with cane syrup eggs, butter, cream, and milk, I, aged fourteen, milked two or three cows. That project included allowing the calves to suckle their mother a bit. Then rope the calf and tie it to the fence nearby. Return to the cow and milk her. Release the calf and let it continue to nurse its mother. Repeat this process for both cows to be milked. If there were more cows producing milk, the number could be as high as five. Upon completion of milking, I carried the buckets of milk to the kitchen, strained the milk into containers, ceramic or stainless steel. By this time, Minnie and John D had arisen and Minnie joined in the care of the milk. This was usually about two gallons of milk. This process took about forty minutes.

I returned to the barnyard, which we called the "lot," a term simply referring to the piece of ground fenced in to be used to contain the various animals. While I was separating cows and calves, Frank was back at the barn harnessing the mule or mules to be used that day.

We returned to the house for breakfast. After bathing and changing into school clothes, I went back outside and took a bucket of water from the well to the pen where we had a hog for fattening. Fed the pig the leftovers from meals, which were kept in a container set aside for that purpose.

We called that container the "slop bucket" because it was composed of anything thrown away that was edible to a pig, an animal with a broad taste.

Along with the pig, the chickens were watered and fed. When water was carried from the well to the pig, it was carried to the chickens also, as they occupied space that was near the lot.

The cat, a privileged animal, was allowed to come into the house and go out to the yard as it chose. So, the cat was fed in the kitchen. One of the cat's favorite locations was under the cookstove where the floor was warm. Other times, it chose a spot to curl up near the fireplace if it was cold weather.

Goats were kept in a pen with sheds separate from the other livestock. Goats required no attention until noon. Our goats were allowed, by law, as were other barnyard animals, to range freely over the countryside. Our house was surrounded by thousands of acres of cutover pine timberland. This we regarded as free pasture. John D and Minnie had learned that goats, which are browsing animals like deer, rather than grazing animals like cattle and sheep, when released from their pen at noon would go straight to the salt log, lick the salt from the salt notches, and race immediately to the woodlands nearby to browse and wander until evening when they returned home to meet their baby goats, called kids, before nightfall. The mother goats, nannies, would have their udders filled with milk after being away from their kids since noon.

So, the nannies would come home bleating for their kids and the rest of the herd of goats would follow them home. One or more of these older female goats wore bells so we could locate the herd with ease when they were grazing out of sight of the house.

Additionally, the bells served the purpose of letting us know by the sound of the bells whether the goat was grazing, walking, or running. If they were running sometimes, they were being chased by dogs and early rescue had to be arranged immediately.

Using this routine prevented us from having to go so often to the woods and search for the goats to find them and drive them home.

The same routine was used for the milking female cattle.

When dusk was approaching and the men were still working in the fields, schoolchildren had arrived home around 3:30 p.m. on the bus, which we called a "transfer."

Upon arriving home, children changed from their school clothes into work clothes and began helping under parental direction. Ruth, at about age twelve, was singled out as the only girl at home, and from that time on her duties were heavily tilted into activities like food preparation, clothing care sewing, and generally in activities regarded as "women's work." Remember this included milking cows, feeding chickens, raising baby chicks, and gardening.

The dog, in the meantime has been in the yard since the morning. Fed when people eat at mealtime.

The evening milking is to be done late in each day. Minnie was master of ceremonies for feeding and milking the cows. Sometimes Minnie milked the cows, and often she had me perform the chore. Sometimes we both were milking at the same time. My siblings all learned to milk a cow.

Our chickens were housed at the lot, as were most of the other animals. In the evening, the eggs were gathered from the nests which were around the barn.

Exceptions were the cats. One usually stayed at the house and another usually stayed at the barn. Most of the time we kept one dog. The sleeping place of the dog was in a potato shed which contained a bed of deep straw. That was only about fifty feet away from the house so the dog could be called or whistled up in a minute, day or night.

Dogs at the Sylvest homestead never entered the house. When they were tiny puppies, they were kept in the yard. If the puppy climbed the steps and came on the porch, which was about three feet off the ground, the puppy was spanked with a little peach tree switch. By about the third spanking, it learned that it was not welcome to come up on that porch, let alone into the house, day or night.

The exciting times in caring for the animals was when baby animals were being born or hatched and when butchering was going on.

When a hen was ready to "set," meaning she was clucking and ready to set on eggs until they hatched twenty-eight days later, we would place the twenty or so eggs in a nest for the hen to hatch. These exciting times with the animals were excellent times for teaching children about the finer points of caring for the animals.

It was essential that eggs under a setting hen be monitored. When the first egg pipped, that is, when the little hatching chicken inside the egg pecked the shell of the egg and broke it, we all knew that the remaining eggs would hatch within the next twenty-four hours.

When the first egg was pipped, Minnie assigned a child to help build and arrange a coop, a specially made cage in which the mother hen and the baby chicks would be kept. The hen would sometimes be permitted to raise her young in the lot at some risk to losing some chicks to hawks and other predators like snakes, opossums, coons, and mink. Sometimes even a neighbor's dog would raid a hen nest and suck all the eggs.

If it was cold weather, different tactics were called for in the care of baby chicks. Minnie usually took them and the hen and placed them in a cardboard box in her warm kitchen until they were old enough to be turned loose in the barnyard with the other chickens.

Since chickens do not give milk, boiled eggs make an ideal diet for a day old chick. Greens from the garden, usually collard greens or green onions, supplemented their boiled egg diet beginning after about a week. Additionally milk was fed to the baby chicks when it was available.

An interesting time occurred too when it was time to rope a calf, by which I mean tie the rope around the baby calf's neck while it is sucking milk from its mother and pull it away and tie it to a post so you can milk the cow. We pulled the calf to a nearby fence where it could not reach its mother, who was eating her feed from a feed trough about ten feet away.

Roping and tying a calf called for learning to tie a knot that would not slip and choke the calf as it strained and pulled trying to get away. I remember John D showing me how to tie the proper knot. Of course, I promptly forgot how to do it. Soon I was called upon to rope the calf again. I did not tie the knot properly and John D observed my error, shaming me for not knowing how to tie that knot.

From that moment, I learned a valuable life lesson. Once shown by your parent, teacher, or boss on the job how to perform a task, it becomes your duty to study and remember the task. I learned to go to someone who knows and get instructions I could practice. I learned to take responsibility for my own learning process. I learned that neither my parent nor boss can do my learning for me. Take notes, learn how to sketch, and ask questions to enhance your learning curve.

In today's vernacular, "Look it up on the Internet and find out."

We used a pigpen about fifteen by fifteen feet square as an enclosure to put grown woods hogs. "Woods hogs" was the term used to apply to domestic hogs of no special breed. Other names were "piney woods rooter" and "razorbacks." One common reference to the hogs was "range hogs" and "woods hogs."

Characteristics of the woods hogs were that they required more corn to produce a pound of dressed meat. However, when the hogs were turned loose on the open range to reproduce and raise broods of pigs, they were not being fed very much, only enough to keep them gentle. Hence, less total corn was required to raise the pig to adulthood.

The woods hog was only fed when placed in the pen about sixty days before it was fat enough to butcher at a weight of around two hundred pounds. They were survivors.

The woods hog that weighed two hundred pounds on foot (*on foot* means as it stands in the pen) would produce about 133 pounds of dressed pork. This is the size that we strove for at butchering time. We killed about twelve hogs each calendar year.

A particular problem with keeping hogs in a pen for fattening is getting enough water to them. The odor from a pigpen is so strong and objectionable that we always built our pigpen at least two hundred yards from our house. Of course our water well was near our house. So it became my job to haul enough water and deliver it to the hogs. This I did with the aid of a mule-drawn sled, which we called a slide. I put a fifty-five-gallon barrel on the slide, hitched a mule to the slide, and drove the rig a quarter mile to the nearest spring. Dipped about forty gallons of water from the spring, poured it into the barrel, and drove the rig to the hog pen.

Again, I had to dip the water from the barrel and pour it over the fence into the trough from which the pigs drank.

Hog killing time for me each year was a relief. I was relieved because I no longer had to haul that barrel of water every day to those hogs.

Draft and saddle animals called for special care, as did all the other farm species. It required more grain for the draft animal when it was working daily than when it was allowed to graze idly in the pasture.

Our saddle mount usually was not used as much as a draft animal as were the other horses and mules, as we desired that it be fully rested before being used as a mount.

During my senior year in high school at Provencal, I rode a white mare to school each day, five miles each way, so I could be home earlier to do more farmwork. I usually got home about 1:00 p.m., and the school bus did not reach the homestead until about 4:00 p.m.

The name of the mare was Mix, so named after Tom Mix who was one of the stars in cowboy movies of the time. Tom Mix always rode a white horse, so we chose Mix as the name of our white horse.

I still miss the animals that went along with everyday living during the Depression.

However, don't forget the good old days are right now, computer and all.

# CHAPTER 29
# Food by the Season

The food for consumption during any season of the year during of the Great Depression was controlled by the weather and methods used to preserve food from one season to the other.

When electricity and refrigeration were not available, there were limited ways of preserving food. Salt was used as a preservative. Sugar was another preservative.

Sterilization of food then sealing it in containers, glass jars of metal cans was also used. Drying was often used.

The major controlling element was the weather, which changed from one season to the next.

Fresh food was almost totally controlled by the weather. Woe to the subsistence farmer who forgot to plant his peas or corn at the proper time, because it could mean crop failure resulting in having to do without the produce from that crop until the following year.

John D and Minnie had planting dates memorized. They were often consulted by young neighbors about what to plant when. This kind of consultation went on after Sunday school and church on Sundays.

Beginning at the first of each year, the first thing planted in the New Year was corn and potatoes in late February. During January and February, our diet often included collard greens, turnip greens, turnips, mustard greens, green onions, and cornbread from corn grown the preceding year. Sugarcane syrup cooked by John D from cane grown on the farm was available the entire year. Milk from cows managed by Minnie and John D was available the entire year. Sweet potatoes from the previous year's crop were available until about March 15. The sweet potatoes were stored in bunks made of pine straw entirely surrounding the potatoes. The pine straw kept the potatoes from freezing.

The pine straw bunk was covered with a makeshift cover of wood or tin to keep out the rain. Sometimes the storage was in small outhouses built for that purpose. When I was a youngster, we had two such potato houses. Each house was a miniature log cabin with a conventional roof of homemade cypress shingles. A pan of baked sweet potatoes was kept present in our kitchen seven days a week. These were used for between meal snacks and as snacks to have along with you when your day's activity was located on remote parts of the homestead.

Canned goods preserved on the farm were consumed all winter. Peaches, blackberries, huckleberries, apples, pears, plums, and strawberries were canned as preserves, with a minimum of sugar, or as jams or jellies cooked with enough sugar to make a heavy syrup. Vegetables were preserved in glass jars. Tomatoes, peas, green beans, and corn were canned in glass jars. Cucumbers were pickled in vinegar and preserved in glass jars. Beets were preserved sometimes in vinegar as pickles and sometimes plain in glass jars.

Onions were protected from freezing by bunking them in pine straw in the manner of sweet potatoes. Green peas, which had been planted in October, began producing green peas for picking in early spring.

In the spring, the broad-leafed plants and root crops, which were planted in the fall, produced abundantly for the daily table. Turnips, cabbage, collards, mustard, lettuce, spinach, beets, and carrots were plentiful.

One of the first vegetables in the garden to become available for the table in the spring was winter-growing green peas, which we knew as "English peas."

Our breakfast table in the spring had milk, cream, butter, syrup, either ham or bacon, biscuits or cornbread, and gravy made from the fat resulting from frying the ham or bacon. Fruit preserves were usually offered: figs, peaches, pears, apples, plums, blackberries, or huckleberries, depending upon the relative abundance of each on hand.

The noon meals in the spring contained cornbread, cooked greens of some variety, a substantial pot of rice, and either of several varieties of beans (pinto, navy, red kidney, butter beans, both speckled and lima varieties) or peas (black-eyed, purple hull, lady finger, black crowders).

Fresh vegetables from the spring garden began to add variety to the above as early as they began to mature. By early April, we could grapple potatoes from under those planted in February. Green onions and other greens from the garden were still available.

By May, we began to pick green snap beans from the garden along with the root crops, carrots, beets, and radishes.

About every two weeks, we would butcher a goat, which provided about twenty pounds of meat. This provided protein rich meat for stews, hash, roasts, soups, and gravies, which, with the milk, eggs, and vegetables, made for a well-balanced diet.

Summer meals were filled with the abundance of all the produce described in the above sections, as summer was the time when the harvesting and preserving took place. Added to the above were all the watermelons, cantaloupes, and muskmelons. Vegetables and fruits preserved by canning and crops preserved by drying laid up the stores which would last through the following winter. This activity continued through the summer and fall.

There was no shortage of food or nutrition during summer and fall when all the preparation for the following winter was going on.

Trimmings and leftovers were used to feed and fatten the pigs, which were being grown to produce the hogs to be butchered and cured in the fall.

By the end of the summer, around the last week in September, we often caught about ten one-year-old pigs from our wild-range hogs and put them into a fattening pen about fifteen feet square. There we fed them and watered them daily on a diet of corn plus greenery vegetable matter to balance the diet, such as sweet potato vines, collard greens, cabbage, watermelons, or any green-foliage crop or vegetable of which we had an abundance. Sweet potatoes provided an abundant supplement to the corn.

By December 1, our pigs were fat and we awaited the first heavy freeze as the chosen time to butcher the hogs. When that decision was made, other activities were put on hold to the fullest extent possible so we could focus on the heavy labor activity of butchering and curing our upcoming year's supply of bacon and hams. This was accompanied by the rendering of fat, which was stored as well.

Late fall and early winter also included completion of the harvest of peanuts, cotton, beans, sweet potatoes corn, and fall Irish potatoes.

I can remember well, as a new season approached, longing for the arrival of the ripening of the crops, which was so appreciated on the table at mealtime.

What could be better than the first of season-ripe watermelon? Or what could taste better than the season's first serving of the new corn crop? And how could anything compete with the fresh pork which resulted from the first pig killed in the fall of the year? The latter was so rewarding that I usually had the pleasure of getting on a mule and riding for three hours to deliver to the homes of four neighbors of whom each was the recipient of a package of fresh pork designated just for that household.

Managing the food supply for regular meals was a challenge to my mother. Providing an adequate, steadily available supply of stored and preserved food for a whole family was a challenge to my father.

We hunkered down during the Great Depression and made it by sharing food, clothing, and shelter with family members and neighbors.

Hunkering down and subsistence living would make a valuable curriculum.

# CHAPTER 30
# Sounds of the Great Depression

The sounds you heard on the Sylvest homestead during the Great Depression and how you interpreted them defined the times and how you were fitting into them.

The household sounds with which I grew up made a deep impression on me. That was before we had the radio, telephone, television, most motor vehicles, airplanes, and police sirens. This was before we had the hum of refrigerator in the kitchen, the whine of the air-conditioning units, the roar of airplane engines overhead, or the sound of jets breaking the sound barrier, which have come to be part of the twenty-first century noise pollution.

Oh! It was not totally silent, because we lived on the farm with plenty of animals around.

Our neighbors, who were all more than one-quarter of a mile away, had the same. The most improved highway in hearing distance was a graveled road one mile from our house, and we could hear every single automobile that traveled over that road. Mufflers were not as effective on automobiles of the 1920s and 1930s as they are today. Sounds of the tires of automobiles on gravel is loud when not drowned out by other sounds.

Household members had their characteristic sounds, from the youngest with their baby crying to the oldest with their grunts and groans, with all of the playing, hazing, chasing, whistling, and singing from those of the age groups in between.

Then there was the friendly sounds of my mother's voice as she soothed me and consoled me when I had pain. When she hummed and sang familiar tunes as she rocked me when I was sleepy. Her daily singing, as she went about her household and garden activities, was the most pleasant sounds a child could hear coming from the person who was still the most important one in the world.

Each animal had its own noisy way of declaring its hunger or other need. Not only did we hear our own animals, we heard the animals that belonged to our neighbors.

From the day I was born, I began learning all the various sounds and their meanings. My ability to interpret the sounds developed over the years until it was possible for me to estimate the time of day by the sounds I could hear.

As a baby, I recall knowing the sounds of my mother's footsteps as they resounded from our wooden floors which were about three feet off the ground. There were a few squeaky boards in the floors of our old sawmill shack, and by the time I could run around the house at age three or four, I had every one of the sounds of those squeaky boards memorized. Every other household member did too. That was helpful knowledge if you were three years old, in your sick bed, and forbidden to get out. From those sounds, you could tell which household member was moving in the house, where he or she was located in the house, and which direction he or she was going.

Add to those floor sounds the sounds of the different voices that were speaking and the words they were saying. Interpreting these sound patterns was as natural as getting a drink of water when you are thirsty.

Beginning early in the day, before the sun rose in the morning, one of the early sounds I remember was the crowing of the rooster in the barnyard. Each farm had about twenty to forty chickens. This meant that each farm had several roosters. All of them crow to announce the beginning of the day. The literal message there is that the roosters crow. Hens (i.e., the female chickens, which lay the eggs) do not crow. I thought maybe I should insert that phrase in case anyone ever reads this book who doesn't know that already.

By the time I could walk, I knew that the crowing of the roosters meant that daylight was soon to follow, getting out of bed would follow that, caring for the animals and kitchen activity would follow that, praying the grace before meals would come next, and finally the meal. Then off to school or work as the individual responded.

The accompanying sounds went along with the activities that were going on in the sequence described.

For example, when the first of Minnie's roosters crowed daily, about 4 a.m., you could predict with unfailing accuracy that Rosette McGaskey's rooster would answer, followed in some random order by the roosters of Aunt Allie Brister, Algy Foshee, Belle Foshee, Lottie Kay, and Lettie Honeycutt. Those ladies, hostesses of the respective households, deserve to be the persons who are recognized as the owners of the roosters, as the chicken project was considered their domain.

Their husbands will be honored elsewhere, so their practice of walking through each other's crops on Sundays with their hands crossed behind their backs during the inspection, displaying the mode of "a not working on Sunday" imbedded habit within the culture which had not yet heard of the expression "round the clock shift work."

Back to the roosters. Oh, yes, indeed, I could name the owner of at least half of the roosters crowing in the morning.

The roosters have merely been taken as a sample of the animal sounds of the morning. As the day progressed, additional sounds from other animals drowned out those of the most distant roosters.

The cows with full udders were mooing, or lowing as we called it, announcing to the world and to their calf that they were ready for that baby calf to be allowed to suck its nourishment. When the owner relented and permitted the cow to enter the enclosure where the calf was, the cow looked around anxiously for the feed that she expected to be in her trough. In the meantime, as she consumed her feed, the calf was making rewarding sucking sounds as it sucked milk from the teats of its mother. Cows have four teats. The calf learns to move from one teat to the other until it drinks all the milk or fills its stomach. Goats, however, have only two teats as do horses.

In the meantime, the cow milker, often me as soon as I was old enough, will have roped the calf and milked the cow by squeezing each teat to expel the milk into a bucket. Our cows typically yielded about two gallons of milk each per day.

The sound of the milk stream hitting the bottom of the empty bucket was a distinctive sound, recognized by all family members in hearing distance. As the amount of milk grew in the bucket, the sound of the milk striking the milk contained there no longer sounded the same as when the milker started.

Another sound that accompanied the milking process was the cow, from whom the calf had been restrained by a rope, turning her head toward her calf to see that it was all right and made a gentle mooing sound inviting the calf, once freed from the rope, to return to the baby-feeding process. Sometimes the calf would bleat loudly, protesting being removed from its teat.

As these sounds could be heard as far away as the hundred yards to our house, my parents could tell if the chores being performed in the lot were progressing well and how nearly the task of milking was to being finished for that time. Milking and feeding of animals took place two times each day.

Mixed in with all these sounds would be the whistling to the dog to get the dog to come and chase an unwanted animal away from where it was interfering with the husbandry taking place. The dog might be heard to bark. The household member in the barnyard might issue more commands to the dog or to the other animals.

Concurrently, the sounds of a fieldworker getting the team ready by feeding and harnessing them could be heard as well as the commands of the voice of the drover. The rattling of the chains in the harness of the work animals was clear and distinct.

This was taking place early in the day. At about the same time in the morning, around 7:00 a.m., the school bus would be departing from Provencal, where Ernest Bell, the school bus driver, lived. Upon departing, Provencal Mr. Bell would let loose with a couple of three-second blasts of his exhaust whistle (illegal nowadays), a sounding and resounding not unlike a locomotive to announce to all families with schoolchildren on his route to get ready to get on the bus.

About fifteen minutes later, the hum of the bus engine would be heard again as the bus approached our homestead, where it turned around at the end of its route, loaded all children at that spot, and departed for the school at Provencal, stopping at each homestead byroad along the way to allow all schoolchildren to board. The bus made a peculiar sound as it hit a loose board when it crossed Corral Branch on a bridge one-quarter of a mile from our house. We all recognized that sound and knew how much longer it would be before the bus arrived at our stop.

The sounds of the school bus as these operations were performed provided a background to all in hearing distance, about two miles.

In the meantime, if the sounds of the wagon began to appear amid the quiet, all in hearing distance knew that the team was pulling the wagon that day to do some needed work of hauling. The sounds of a wagon being pulled by a team is distinctive. Wagons were standard. They all had wheels of wood with metal rims called tires, unlike the rubber inflatable tires of your twenty-first-century automobile, which we love to call "our car," *car* bring short for word *carriage*, which it replaced along with the horse that pulled the carriage.

Wagon sounds could be heard for a mile. The wheels made a heavy hammering sound as the wheels slid, each, boxing on thimble, from side to side, and banged, boxing on thimble, like a heavy hammer. In the front of the wagon, where the tongue, doubletree, and singletrees were attached to the front axle of the wagon, were the "hounds" where the wagon tongue was fastened to the front axle with a sort of hinge with a heavy rod running through it.

As the tongue of the wagon slid from side to side on this rod, the tongue banged sharply and loudly against the other part of the hinge. The noise thus made was called the "barking of the hounds," as the sound closely resembled the sound of a large dog barking.

The barking of the hounds could be heard a great distance. Each wagon had its own characteristic sound, which changed as the vehicle went from turf, to hard ground, to gravel, and to hard surface.

The owner of the wagon could be recognized by those familiar with it just by the sound. The weight of the load could be estimated to some extent by the sound as a fully loaded wagon makes different sounds from an empty wagon. When a moving wagon is unloaded, it rattles more and makes more hollow sounds. Also, the team pulling a loaded wagon will proceed more slowly than a lightly loaded wagon.

After the morning milking, feeding of animals, breakfast, and departure of family members, the sounds of the day change as the household settles down to being just the mother and preschool-age children. Little ones expect more attention. They also look forward to more adventures, for as their mother brings them along to the garden where she is picking beans or greens, the youngsters enjoy the outdoor sounds, the northern mockingbird singing in the nearby fig tree, northern cardinals with high-pitched peeps and their nest in a plum tree, and the purple martins, with their constant chirping as they go in and out of the homemade bird house mounted on a tall pole in the yard.

In the distance can be heard the steam whistle of Weaver Brothers Lumber Company sawmill about four miles away at Flora, Louisiana, announcing that it is noontime.

Sometimes when that whistle blew, a household member would go quickly to our clock in the living room on the mantelpiece over the fireplace and set the clock to 12:00 noon. That is the means we had of correcting our time when the winding clocks, the only kind we had, would run down from untimely winding or just lose the correct time because they ran either too slow or too fast. They sounded the same in either case. The sound of the clock on our mantel could be heard in each bedroom when the house was otherwise quiet at night. The ticking of the clock was peaceful and reassuring.

What was going on outside in the vicinity of the homestead could be monitored by the sounds heard. We knew that a cow was in heat somewhere nearby when we heard the familiar deep-pitched bellow of the range bull as he approached in search of his ladylove, which just might be the cow you are planning to milk. In that event, you knew to stay away from the vicinity of the cow in question, because until that bull had finished with his courtship, valentine giving, and otherwise lovemaking, he was no creature to mess with. The lady was his property alone, and he would chase anyone in the vicinity over the fence with no questions asked. We learned at an early age that love is blind but mad bulls are not, and we could tell they were mad by the bellowing sounds they made.

They were the most dangerous of our domestic animals, not to minimize the sometimes fierceness of horses, mules, and hogs.

Other animal sounds would take place that characterized the time of day. Since our fields were as far as one-half mile from our house, when noontime came and my mother was ready to call workers to the house to eat at mealtime she took a hunting horn which hung on a nail in the wall in our hallway. Minnie could mortally blow that horn. You could hear it for at least a mile. It was her signal for farmworkers to interrupt what they were doing and assemble at our kitchen dining table for "dinner," the meal we served at noon. The evening meal was called "supper."

Other times that horn was blown were when an emergency was to be announced. On that occasion, the horn was blown three long blasts. A few seconds were allowed to lapse and the horn was again blown three long blasts. All families in the neighborhood knew that emergency signal. Not only were there no cell phones, there were no phones.

I remember one occasion when that horn was blown. Retha Masters, who was two years old at the time, a little neighbor who was visiting with us with her family, had disappeared. Retha was the child of Jefferson Masters and Jane Honeycutt Masters. When her family and ours realized that Retha could not be found on our homestead, John D blew that horn three times. Then he took his shotgun, a twelve-gauge, double-barreled hammer gun, from its rack above the mantelpiece and fired it into the air three times. After about three minutes, he fired that shotgun three more times.

These were truly sounds of the times because neither of these means of communicating an emergency would be recognized in the twenty-first century culture.

After firing the gun, he put me on a mule to ride to the neighbors to tell them Retha was lost.

It was about two hours before we received news that Retha had been found. That two-year-old had walked alone about two miles from our house to a spot north of Horsepen Creek near the Longino homestead, nearly halfway from our house to Provencal. Someone found her lying down sleeping on a small sandbar in the roadside ditch and began searching for her family so they could return her to them.

At the all clear announcement, the hunting horn was again blown three times, a minute was allowed to lapse and it was blown three times, the signal recognized at the time as the all clear. The shotgun was again fired into the air three times, a minute or so was allowed to lapse, and it was fired three times again, the signal recognized at the time as the all clear announcement.

When such a signal was being sent out, everyone in hearing distance repeated the signal. It is amazing how such emergencies could be announced and spread over a ten-mile area in only minutes.

After the all clear was sounded and some days had passed, I overheard a conversation between two of our neighbors describing the search for Retha. George Slaughter, of Vowells Mill, Louisiana, said he was out walking the roads searching for Retha for so long and his feet were so tired that when they passed each other one foot would say, "If you'll let me by this time, I'll let you by next time."

Retha was unharmed, and happy parents and neighbors celebrated.

The sounds of midday after the blowing of the horn at dinnertime changed from those of the morning. In the morning, both people and animals were arising from their night's rest, all were present, and after the morning routine was done, all went about their day's activities.

After lunch could come the rest time for small children who were young enough to be required to take a nap. At this time, my mother would sometimes lie down with the children in order to get them to calm down enough for their fatigue to make them go to sleep. As soon as the children were asleep, she would arise and return to her duties. That was one busy lady.

At noontime each day, a family member old enough to salt the goats would take about a cup of salt and distribute about a teaspoonful into each notch, of which there were about twenty-five in a forty-foot log or one notch about every twelve inches. After distributing the salt, the person would go open the hatch, a small elevated doorway (elevated about twenty inches so the baby goats could not jump out and follow their mothers into the woods and get lost) in the fence of the goat pen, and the goats would stream out into the open area of about two acres in front of our house and race as fast as they could run to the salt log, knowing that the salt would be there. The goats, who loved salt, rapidly licked all the salt from the log and within five minutes went racing after their leaders toward the surrounding woods to browse on buds and small leaves on low-growing vegetation. The sound of the little goat bells would resound to the surrounding area as the goats went hurriedly and competitively from plant to plant and went farther from home until the bells could barely be heard. Sometimes they would go a mile away, a distance over which we could not hear their bells.

If it was getting late in the day and we could not hear one of the goat bells, someone, usually a child, was sent to walk out in different directions to listen for the goat bells. When they heard the bell and found the goats, they drove them home to be penned at night. The family dog was trained to manage the goats and drive them home.

As the herd of goats approached the homestead late in the day, the baby goats, called kids, which had been kept penned up since noon while the adult goats were out feeding, would hear the goat bell and know that their mothers were coming home to them. We kept the kids penned up during the day precisely so their mothers would return home for the night where they were safe. The little goats started bleating, and when their mothers got close enough to hear them there was a scramble to see which goat could jump back through the hatch into the pen. There was also a plethora of mother goats bleating for their babies.

Once nanny and kid were reunited, it was fun to watch the delighted baby goats nurse their mothers. Each mother goat knew the smell of her baby and would not let another baby goat come to her and nurse. Likewise, each baby goat knew the smell of its mother and went only to her. There was considerable confusion when the herd of adult goats and kids were first reunited. Not all the mothers could leap through the hatch door at one time. Although it appeared that they were trying. The kids whose mothers were the last ones to get through the door were anxiously searching among the twenty or so other mothers for their own. Within a few minutes, all the bleating ceased and the pandemonium ended for the night. By the time the sun was down, all the goats were resting, contentedly sleeping under the sheds in their pen which were put there for that purpose.

As the late day sounds of the goats went through the evening portion of its cycle, so did the sound of the cows and calves. Calves *baaing* for their mothers and cows *mooing* for their calves. After the milking cows were milked and the calves had nursed, we could hear the commands of one or more family members driving each individual animal into the section of the barnyard where it was directed to go for the night.

The typical arrangement was for the cows to be kept in the cow pen and the calves released into an adjacent pasture area.

Other end-of-the-day sounds were the chickens being called before sundown, where they were fed corn. I recall taking a half dozen ears of corn from the crib, removing the shucks, and shelling the corn on to the ground as all the chickens scrambled to eat every bit of it before the others got to it.

As sundown approached, the clucking and chuckling sounds of the chickens could be heard as each one made its way into the chicken house and up to the roosting bars where they would roost for the night.

Minnie's voice could be heard also as she told one or more children to go get the eggs so they would not be left in the nests over night.

Other parental commands closed down the day, instructing responsible parties just what to do that got the entire population of animals of the barnyard secure for the night.

Then all residents of the household assembled for supper when it was almost dark.

A background of value for a lifetime is the music made at our homestead. Daily, we sang the gospel songs which we heard at church on Sunday and at the Sylvest homestead on Wednesday nights, which were dedicated to singing songs around the piano with an occasional rendition or concert of sorts by a family member who played another instrument, such as a guitar, harmonica, or violin.

By the time I finished high school, I had learned enough of the gospel songs in the Baptist hymnals that sometimes on Sundays I would lead the congregation in the singing for the church services. So could either of my four brothers, depending upon which one was present.

My mother and five sisters all played the piano and the pump organ and sang. This acceptance of my nonprofessional music efforts sustained me during my lifetime with the appreciation that enabled me to join Eloise, my wife, in nourishing the musical talents of our seven children.

Those good sounds began at a very early age at the Sylvest homestead at Provencal.

Different groups from the family, not to exclude guests who were talented, and so inclined, sang and played music every Wednesday night for years on end.

Another group of sounds which impacted our life was the sounds of weather.

The sounds of weather were well known and studied at home. Each morning, the appearance of the atmosphere was evaluated to see if any weather conditions were a threat to the desired activities of the day. The most disturbing event that upset a day's activities was rain. Sometimes it rained for days. Other times, it remained dry for months with almost no rain. Either extreme was disruptive. Rain was certainly not desired in quantities in the spring planting season to the extent of interfering with the planting process.

A remark commonly heard describing the dialogue relating to the weather would go like this: "Well," John D would say, "son, it is too wet to plow today, so you and Royce go cut that little red oak by the pasture gate and begin splitting it up for stove wood."

The reply from Thomas Ard, yours truly, was, "Yes, sir."

Believe me: the sounds of the place and time made an impact that you remembered forever if it was the sound of your father's voice giving an order which you must execute.

As a child, I can remember racing to the protection of the barn, if that was the closest shelter when rain began to fall. One could get caught under the shed at the barn and be kept there for an hour waiting for the rain to slack up enough to permit a race to the house to keep from getting wet. The sound of the rain hitting the roof of the barn had its distinct music. Wood shingles muffled the sound of the raindrops. Corrugated metal roofs magnified and resounded the sounds of the falling rain.

Our house had a solid cypress shingle roof on it when I was a teenager in the 1930s and 1940s. We had a gutter the length of the house in a hallway which collected water to make it run into a barrel at the end of the hallway in our backyard.

The sound of the water pouring into the barrel was not unlike a small waterfall. And the rain running off the roof into the galvanized gutter made music of its own,

As our house was quite open, without glass windows, when thunder occurred it was easy to hear it. There really was no such thing as sleeping through a thunderstorm unless you were extremely tired. The sounds of the weather touched the life of every family member.

Other sounds that we were exposed to during our workday were the unheard of, unthought of sounds that were close to each activity in which we engaged. One of those was the sounds of the footsteps of our mounts when we were riding horse or mule. If we were fortunate enough to have a saddle, we heard the squeaking of the leather saddle from the moment we mounted until the moment when our feet were next on the ground.

The jingle of the bits on the bridle of the horse as the animal strode along, whatever gait the horse was in, a walk, trot, or gallop. No two bridles had the same ring and jingle.

The *clop clop* of the feet of the horse was unique as it stepped on hard ground or in gravel. This sound was affected by the condition of the shoes on the horse, if indeed it had shoes, which was not always the case. It was also affected by whether or not the ground was wet from rain or dry from drought.

As the Depression years reached the late 1930s, it was more and more frequently that we heard the sound of an airplane overhead. Occasionally we would see an airplane passing overhead. Usually it was a biplane, which had come to Natchitoches to take passengers for a ride for a dollar at the Natchitoches Parish Fair each October.

Yes, the sounds of the Great Depression are stamped in my memory along with the taste of cornbread on my palate.

And now, I listen to the sound of my cell phone as it lifts me into the present and out of the sounds of my memory.

# CHAPTER 31
# Uncommon Food Preparation

Discussion of dishes and ways of preparing food to meet special needs comes up often in conversation about living in the piney woods during the Great Depression.

## Milk Products

Whole milk was available for cooking, drinking, and processing into other dairy products. On our farm, we separated cream by setting the milk aside overnight so the cream could rise to the top. Then we skimmed the cream from the top of the milk with a large spoon and deposited the cream into a ceramic churn. When the right amount of cream was accumulated to churn, from half to three-quarters full, we churned the sour cream until the butter aggregated into lumps separating it from the milk. Sometimes we consumed the cream as sour cream, very good for cooking or for eating. It was especially good with cane syrup.

When milk was brought into the house after milking was done each morning and evening, if the weather was cold, the milk was put into covered containers. We had several crocks we filled each day and covered with the cloth from washed and bleached flour sacks made of white cotton muslin. After spreading the cloth cover over the container of milk, a string was tied around it to hold the cloth in place. This prevented insects from flying into the container. Sometimes the container was covered by placing a ceramic table plate on it as a lid.

Where the milk was placed for it to cool depended upon the season of the year and the outside temperatures. Milk fresh from the cow is warm, being the precise temperature of the cow. It gradually cooled during the milking and handling. Additional steps were taken as the weather dictated to cool the milk as soon after milking as possible. Warm milk will begin to sour (ferment) rapidly at room temperature. We had shelved space screened in special-built cabinets to keep flies and moths away from the milk and all other food.

During the warm months of spring, summer, and early autumn, we usually put the milk container in a bucket and lowered it into our well until it was just above the water. Our well was fifty feet deep, and the temperature of the water was a nearly constant sixty-five degrees. In this manner, we kept our milk from souring immediately and thus had whole sweet milk to drink each meal.

## Cottage Cheese

Fresh milk was strained through a cheesecloth type of material which often was a flour sack of muslin. We used the same strainers in which to put clabber, soured skimmed milk which had formed a solid curd. By pouring the clabber into the muslin cloths, made into a sort of sack strainer, and hanging the sack from an overhead support, a nail driven into a rafter, if on the porch or from a ceiling hook with a cord tied to it so it could be reached by a person standing on the floor in the kitchen.

A sack filled with clabber and hung over a bowl to catch the whey which dripped from it over night would retain a gallon of milk solids, which we know as cottage cheese. It was a favorite food at our house though not all households used the procedure.

It was used to consume as it came from the strainer. Sometimes we ate it with cane syrup poured over it. Sometimes it was served with fresh or canned fruit as available, preserves, jelly, or jam. On occasion, it became part of a fruit salad with cottage cheese.

## Butter

Making butter is not a difficult process. We allowed the cream to rise for a few hours on fresh milk. Then we skimmed the cream off with a large spoon and accumulated it in my mother's ceramic churn, a container of approximately two gallons capacity. When the churn was about half full, it was ready to be churned.

The accumulation of the gallon of cream required about two or three days. We did not always skim the cream from all the milk. Rather we skimmed enough to make butter when we chose.

It was a peaceful picture to me as a child to look at my mother sitting in her special straight-backed, cowhide-bottomed chair with her Bible in her lap, her churn of cream setting on the floor beside her chair near her right hand, the dasher in her right hand which moved the dasher up and down, up and down, stroke after stroke, as she turned the pages of her Scripture with her left. Sometimes she had another book in her lap, and sometimes she was holding a baby, child, grandchild, or neighbor instead.

About an hour's moving of the paddle up and down, with about a six-inch stroke, would cause the butterfat in the milk to stick together in the form of lumps of butter. When this occurred, it was said to have "gathered." When gathered, it could be dipped out of the churn and put into a bowl. Rinsing the butter in the bowl by pouring cold water over it and letting the water overflow as the butter was stirred removed the residual milk from the butter making it almost pure butter. In fact, it was ready for market or consumption as desired.

While butter was a delicacy sought after by all cooks, it was difficult to preserve or transport without refrigeration during hot weather. On occasion, my mother would get a request for a pound of butter from a schoolteacher. In that case, she would make the butter and mould it in her butter mould. The butter mould held exactly one pound of butter. When the mould was filled and the pasty butter was packed down in the mould, the little design of a flower with four petals would imprint itself in the top of the pound of butter as it fell from the mould. One of Minnie's school children riding the school bus to Provencal to school would deliver the butter to the teacher who would arrange for the butter to be taken to her house nearby and placed in her "ice box." Again, no refrigeration because residents of Provencal did not have electricity during the Great Depression or during WW II. An ice truck from Natchitoches, Louisiana, the parish seat (Louisiana has parishes, not counties) delivered ice to Provencal two days each week. Possibly 5 percent of the households of Provencal purchased ice, as the rest could not afford it. As I recall, a twenty-five-pound block of ice cost a nickel. Who had a nickel to pay for it?

Since we had an abundance of milk most of the time, we made as much butter as we chose and consumed the other milk products as well. Other milk products included sweet cream, sour cream, whole milk, buttermilk, and whey. While whey contains a valuable amount of protein, we did not consume it at the table; rather, we used it for animal feed for chickens and hogs.

Our market for butter was so limited that we seldom made butter for sale. It was an item used as a perishable delicacy to be shared with neighbors when in abundant supply, as butter was a favorite ingredient in cake recipes. The community rule of thumb was to share perishables you have in abundance before they spoil and go to waste.

## Corn

Corn was a staple and foundational crop in the piney woods during the Great Depression.

For food, the primary form in which corn was used was as corn meal. Hence, I went to the corncrib each week and shucked and shelled as much corn as required to supply our household with corn meal for the week forthcoming. That was typically one-half a bushel, otherwise described as two pecks or four gallons. That is quite a bit of work for one teenage boy on a weekly basis.

Other forms of corn for table consumption included the corn picked from the stalks when the developing grains were in the "dough stage" of maturity. More specifically, when the grains were still so soft that if the grain were pressed with a thumbnail the juice inside the grain would burst forth in a small stream of white liquid resembling milk. This was the field test we were all taught to perform when harvesting corn for "roasting ears" to be boiled or roasted on the cob. We used the same test as a guide if we were harvesting the corn to be cut off the cob with a knife so the kernels would fall free as whole grains of corn. A third way of harvesting and preparing the fresh corn was to cut the tops off the grains of corn and scrape the cob, removing most of the remainder of each grain as a paste. This was used to make a delicious table dish of "scraped corn."

If, near the end of the crop year, we were short of corn in the crib from the previous year's crop, we used the means above to begin eating our current corn crop to reduce the rate of consumption from the crib supply to make it last longer.

Another problem that could come close to home regarding corn and corn meal was when the gristmill was out of service for any reason. Henry McGaskey probably was the most reliable gristmill operator. Few times do I recall him not grinding corn on Saturday fifty-two weeks of the year. When that happened, I recall that Minnie, my mother, took about a gallon of shelled corn and poured it into a two-gallon container. She then covered the corn with water nearly to the top of the container, took about three tablespoons of lye (sodium hydroxide) crystals, and added them to the water. This procedure was not unlike soaking beans to have them swell for cooking. However, in the case of the corn, the lye was added to the water to loosen the skin on each grain of corn when it swelled to full size. The corn was then rinsed with an abundance of water and the remaining corn was separated from the husks, which were fed to the hogs.

The "lye hominy" which resulted was ready for seasoning and boiling just as it was. It could further be mixed with other ingredients to make various lye hominy dishes to eat while we had no corn meal available from the gristmill. Sometimes we mixed the hominy with meat or made a gravy to go with it.

There were times when we did not have the lye. At those times, we kept out ashes from the two fireplaces in the house and dumped them into a fifty-five-gallon wooden barrel. When the barrel was about one-third full, John D, my father would pour a bucket of water over the ashes to keep them wet. From a bung hole at the bottom of the barrel would flow a small drip or stream of dark brown liquid. We caught this liquid in a container and stored it. The liquid was a satisfactory substitute for lye.

The crystalline form of lye we obtained from Provencal, which had three general stores. We exchanged a dozen eggs for a can of lye at one of the stores.

## Gathering Food from the Wild

Both plant and animal products which grew wild in the piney woods were relied upon to some extent on a steady basis. Cows, hogs, and goats were basic animals which lived in the piney woods even though they were domesticated. They were fed as necessary and housed or penned when the need arose or the season dictated.

One wild plant on which we relied regularly was the blackberry. In a typical year, we would pick and preserve up to twenty gallons. During the picking season, we cooked and ate many on a regular basis. They are excellent for making jam and jelly and for use in cooking pies and cobblers. They may be used for making wine, which was not done in that staunch Southern Baptist household.

One summer in the mid 1930s, we assembled galvanized porcelain and wooden containers and loaded them on our wagon pulled by two mules. Four adults, including Algy Foshee, Effie Miller, Maureen Foshee, and Weuell Foshee, plus me, loaded on the wagon and drove to the Kisatchie Creek bottom to what we called the old Gibbs place about four miles away. It was an area of abandoned fields. Blackberry bushes were rampant. It was July and nearly one hundred degrees. We picked over twenty gallons of blackberries, hauled them home, and divided them among the families involved just as the sun was going down.

This berry-producing plant has been known and used by mankind for thousands of years. The berries are still good. The berries grew on briars. The roots are perennial and the canes bearing the berries are biennial.

Blueberries were abundant on our farm, which had about one hundred acres of woodland. The plants on which the wild blueberries grew were shrubs which were found along small streams most of the time. The wild blueberries were sweeter than the domestic varieties which produce blueberries for market in the twenty-first century.

The problem with the wild blueberries is that they are small and it takes a lot of time to pick enough berries to fill a gallon container. We typically had about five gallons of preserved blueberries, which we called huckleberries. Frank and Ouida Renner (my mother's sister) transplanted about one hundred wild huckleberry bushes onto their small farm near Franklinton, Louisiana. That shows how much some of the wild plants of our piney woods were used and appreciated.

Plums of numerous varieties were planted on farms in the piney woods. Often the farms were abandoned as the piney woods land is not choice land for growing crops. Being a hardy plant, the plums and occasionally apple, pear, or fig trees remained when the farms were abandoned, and the residents of the area helped themselves to the largesse. We often picked and canned plums as preserves for making pies and cobblers.

Grapes of some varieties grow well in the sandy soils of the piney woods. Many years before the Great Depression, a vineyard of imported grapevines was planted just south of Victoria Station and about four miles west of Provencal.

As a ten-year-old in 1935, I rode on a wagon with family members to the site of hundreds of acres grown over with trees and underbrush but still spotted with dozens of surviving grapevines which freely climbed into trees of all kinds. We were able to harvest about twenty gallons of grapes which we used to make preserved grape juice for wintertime consumption.

In late winter sometimes, we would not have success with winter growing broadleaf greens for home use. I remember accompanying Minnie into the piney woods near our home and searching for poke salad greens and dock, otherwise called wild lettuce. These two wild greens grow all over the piney woods but are not in concentrated patches as in a garden. The consumer of these greens had a lot of walking and searching before locating and picking a gallon for cooking. Either of these greens may be harvested and cooked like collards, spinach, or mustard greens and can be mixed with other such greens. The purpose they served for us was to assure Minnie of the balanced diet for her family. She was keenly aware of the importance of good nutrition, being the granddaughter of a medical doctor who had graduated from Tulane University.

## Peanuts As a Food Item

We grew peanuts to be consumed as food and as feed for livestock. The plants of peanuts were harvested by pulling them up by hand. The entire plant is laid across the row and left there to dry. The peanuts, which grow under the ground, are still attached to the drying peanut vines. The plants were sometimes stacked in shocks in the field and retrieved later.

Sometimes we loaded wagonloads of the whole plants and hauled them to a barn where they were unloaded into the barn with pitchforks. They were safe here from the elements. We would pick the peanuts from the vines when an occasion arose that we wanted some to cook.

Parched peanuts were served as a snack to be taken along by the pocketful when working on the farm. Sometimes we took some in our school lunches. They were often served along with popcorn when parties were held in our house. This took place almost weekly.

Many times, I would be directed to go to the barn where the peanut vines loaded with peanuts were stored to pick two gallons of peanuts in their shells for parching by my older brothers and sisters.

On occasion, we would assemble several family members to work on some food product. The peanut butter project was particularly suited to this procedure, as a lot of time was required to shell enough peanuts to make a gallon of peanut butter.

Once shelled, the parched peanuts were placed in a large metal pan which we called the small dishpan, the name for several such general utility pans in Minnie's kitchen. Someone rubbed the shelled peanuts until the husks came loose. The husks, which are much lighter than the nuts, were separated by winnowing. The pans filled with the nuts with loosened husks were taken outdoors where the husks could be blown away by the wind, if it was blowing. If there was no wind blowing, another member of the household would use a piece of cardboard as a fan and blow the husks away as someone poured the mixed peanuts and husks from a height of about eighteen inches back into the original pan.

This was a short, easy process.

The pan of clean peanuts was then set on a block of wood in the yard and the nuts were pounded with a heavy hammer with a heavy iron head. Actually, the hammer was a coupling pin which had come from the remnants of a logging railroad that had crossed our property. The peanuts rapidly formed a paste as the pounding continued. As the pounding continued and progressed, the paste was stirred and reshaped with a heavy spoon until a smooth finished product of sweet peanut butter was all that remained in the pan. It was then salted to taste and readied for preserving. We removed the peanut butter and stored it in jars.

## Popcorn

Popcorn grows in the field on a stalk like regular corn. The stalks are typically smaller than regular field corn. So are the ears of corn. Popcorn was often thought of as a companion to peanuts because both made good party snacks and they were often served together. That is about the end of their resemblance.

A common variety of popcorn produced ears of corn about one and one-half inches in diameter and eight inches long. The yellow grains had a round crown, as popcorn is classified as "flint corn" unlike the regular field varieties which are known as "dent corn." The crown of the dent corn kernel is indented when it is mature and dry. Sweet corn varieties belong to the dent type. We usually did not shuck and shell field corn or popcorn to store it but simply shucked and shelled enough for the project at hand, such as the supply of corn meal for the week, as it is well suited to being stored in the barn or a container in the shucks.

Another variety of popcorn which we grew regularly was called "rice popcorn." The ears were about two inches in diameter and only about six inches long. The grains were ivory colored like grains of milled rice, hence the name. Either variety was excellent when popped. We grew both for the simple reason that when two kinds are grown, if one crop fails to do well the back-up crop may do better, ensuring an adequate basic supply.

# APPENDIX A
# In Memory of a Slave, Rans McGaskey

By Artie Sylvest Varnado
1993

It was 1916 that my parents, John Dolphus and Minnie Fendlason Sylvest, and their six children moved from Franklinton, Louisiana, to Pineville. We were natives of Washington Parish and we left many relatives there when we moved to live near Louisiana Baptist College in Pineville.

About seven years later, for some reason, my parents moved in March 1923 to Natchitoches Parish and a 160-acre farm that was centrally located among the villages of Provencal, Bellwood, and Vowells Mill, Louisiana. This was soon after World War I had ended and the world was in a financial crisis. This was a time when no jobs could be found and everyone was trying to farm in order to have food to eat. Families shared whatever they had with other needy families. This was hard times. "God was our Great Deliverer" and "His Banner over us was Love." He helped us through it all.

I tell you all of this for, if circumstances had not been this way, I may have never met Rans McGaskey, who is the hero of this story.

When we moved to Provencal, the house we moved into had been built of green, freshly cut, sawed pine boards. The lumber had dried and shrunk and left lots of cracks and open space between the boards. It was really two houses with the bedrooms in one section and the dining room and kitchen in the other section. These were joined by a porch and breezeway between the bedrooms and the kitchen.

Our nearest neighbor was a black family named Henry and Rosette McGaskey, and they had a large family like ours. We thought their house was much better than ours. Henry McGaskey was an intelligent man and a good provider. He was a capable leader in his family, his church, and his community. This law-abiding man was the son of Gus McGaskey who was the son of Rans McGaskey, who was once a slave. Rans reared a family of his own after the emancipation, and Henry was one of the sons of Gus. These families all loved one another and lived near Provencal and tried to share and help each other in times of need.

When old Grandpa Rans was in need of some tender loving care, his grandson Henry took the old man to his home and loved and cared for him until he died. Henry's whole family loved Rans and tried to keep the old man comfortable and happy.

I was fifteen years old when we moved there in 1923, and everyone thought that Rans was about one hundred and three years old at that time. He was a man of medium height and he walked erect except when he leaned on his homemade cane. He was blind but was mentally alert to everything going on around him. He was always clean and neatly dressed and wore comfortable shoes. His white hair and white beard glistened as he walked in the sunshine along the road. I have no memory of him ever using tobacco in any form.

It was always a joy to see Rans coming to our house down a road where wagons, cows, and horses traveled and people walked. His hearing must have been excellent, for he walked through the sandy roadway and never got on the roadside where grass and leaves were. He had to pass near our barns where goats and cows often stood outside the gates, but we always helped him to feel safe and secure, even walking all the way home with many times.

Rans was a great singer, and his songs were filled with rhythm as he would slap his hands and pat his feet while he sang. His songs were those he had sung on the old plantation. We loved them.

Rans frequently spent the day at our house, and he loved to lean back against a chair that was propped against the wall and had a pillow on it for him to lean on. This was in the breezeway where it was cool and he loved to sip his coffee there also.

Besides singing for us, Rans loved to tell us about "when I was a boy." He never said where, but it must have been in a tropical country and near a beach or harbor, for this is how he told it: "I was a boy" (no age or place given) "and I played near the seashore. I saw lots of birds, and my favorite one was the red bird, but every time that I tried to catch one, it always flew away." Evidently, the boats, ships, or canoes that were coming into the harbor or along the seashore were fascinating to Rans. He may have lived in a village near the shore, for he said that one day a ship came close enough to shore that he could see something red on it. He kept wondering about the red. He didn't know what it was, for it never moved. He had never seen anything red except the red bird, and "it always flew away." Apparently, the ship stayed in the harbor or near the seashore for a few days, for Rans said that one day the man from the boat came to him and asked him if he would like to go on the boat to see it better. Rans said, "Yes," and the man took him on the boat. After seeing that the red was not a red bird but a piece of red cloth, the man took Rans down into the hold of the ship where they carried supplies in the bottom of the boat and tied him there. Rans always ended his story with these words: "And I never did see my mama again."

In my deepest secret thoughts, I like to think of Rans as being a beautiful, black-eyed, very young boy not over five or six years old when he was kidnapped to be sold as a slave. This old slave trader was eager to choose the best so he could get more money when he sold one at the auction block—and who wouldn't want to buy a smart, bright-eyed boy to train and maybe to make him an overseer on his plantation? I think the McGaskey family is a family that is proving its worth in the world today. Maybe the high ideals of your family could be traced back to Grandpa Rans.

Our home was a Christian home, and we loved Bible study, hymn singing, telling Bible stories, and praying. This was our witness, and we often invited our neighbors to come and participate with us. Another way Mama witnessed was through her singing. For instance, if Mama was not close enough to talk and a lost person was on the porch, she might sing "Ye Must Be Born Again." Then she might sing "Jesus Is Calling" or "Trust and Obey." She was sowing spiritual seed and trusting God to give the increase.

Rans was very interested in spiritual things. And I think he visited us so often to hear more. After all, Rans had lived more than a century and he knew it would not be long before he would meet Jesus face-to-face. I was just a teenager, but I was a Christian teenager, and I have shared with you my true feelings. I praise God for this opportunity to share with you about one of the best friends I ever had.

# APPENDIX B
# Tractor Accident of J. D. Sylvest: 1944

Following is a letter from Ruth Germaine Sylvest Dear, my younger sister, telling me the story of our father's tractor accident and recovery in 1944 and 1945. I had never heard the details in this story before I received this letter from Ruth the week of 8/1/2006.

The reason I had never heard the details before is that I was in WW II and overseas from the time of the accident until 1946, two years later.

John D Sylvest—Accident—1944

This is the story of my father's accident on our farm in Provencal, Louisiana, in Natchitoches Parish, as I remember it.

It started in May 1944, the day after I graduated from high school, about the middle of May. Late in the afternoon, Papa and Elton got on the tractor and started over to the neighbor's house. Papa had tied a board onto the side of the tractor; it sat on the back axle and was tied to something on top of the engine. Anyway, Elton was driving and Papa was sitting on the board. Praise the Lord, it had been raining and the road was muddy and the ground was soft. They hit a mud hole and Papa fell in it, and the back wheel of the tractor rolled over him, right over his hips and lower internal organs.

It happened near our closest neighbor's house, Mr. Henry McGaskey. They had a pickup truck which they used, picked Papa up, and put him in the cab. Oh, how that must have hurt! I didn't see that part.

This, I did see. You could hear Papa hollering and groaning even before the truck stopped at our front gate.

Our mama got a single bed mattress from the house and had it placed in the bed of the truck. Papa's hips were both crushed, and we could hear what sounded like bones rubbing together when they moved him out of that truck to the mattress.

The two neighbor men got Papa out of that cab and laid him on that mattress.

Mama got her purse and a change of clothes and told Elton and me to take care of things around here while she was gone. She said, "I'll get word to you whenever I can."

I never felt so low.

The truck took our parents away, and all we knew to do was pray. Thank the Lord for praying parents and for teaching us God is near and he hears.

The ambulance came from Natchitoches Parish Hospital and picked up Papa and Mama. Our neighbor stopped by and told us that much.

If I remember right, all of this happened on a Friday night, and we didn't hear anything from them for all of the next week.

I have often wondered if Papa and Mama had any money on them and how Mama managed, being a diabetic. I understand the doctors in Natchitoches called Johnnie and explained Papa's condition and that he needed more help than they could give.

Don't forget this was wartime and gas was rationed, and there were no telephones closer than five miles. We didn't even have electric lights.

Finally, I asked my neighbor if he could go to the hospital and see what he could find out. He came back to tell us they had moved him to Baton Rouge. Later, we got a letter from Mama, praise the Lord.

Pauline was in the service and stationed at Harding Field (in Baton Rouge) at that time. Johnnie was at home with two young children—just babies, really, at this time. So our sister, Pauline, came all the way from Baton Rouge in an ambulance and picked up Papa and Mama and took them to Our Lady of the Lake Hospital up by the state capital.

Around the first of June, Mama came home to see after the farm and sent me down to Johnnie's and the hospital to help out and look after Papa.

Papa was sixty-five years old at the time of the accident and, at first, nobody thought he would make it, let alone walk again. He had a lot of attention. Army doctors and others that Johnnie had worked with or for stopped in, and even the sisters there treated him special and used to ask him if he had any more girls they could train for nurses. Ha!

They wanted to put Papa in a body cast, but he stood his ground. "I'll die if you put me in one of those. I am going to live and walk again," he told everybody who came in. There were so many prayers going up to God for this wonderful father.

I stayed at Johnnie's and caught the city park bus every morning, one block behind Johnnie's house, rode it down town, changed buses at Third Street, and rode on to the lake. Papa is flat on his back with weights on his legs and sand bags all around them. He could reach over his head and lift up his back, somewhere I could rub it good with alcohol, lotion, or just a wet washcloth. I rubbed him all over several times a day.

His room was on the west side of the hospital, so the afternoon sun was kind of warm at times. His room was also set up so he could see down the hall. I would feed him all three meals before I rode the bus back to Johnnie's. I played with Mary Ann and Pauline who was just a baby. Oh, how I loved them.

I kept Papa's feet and legs rubbed good. I did this from June to October, and they took the weights off and moved a hospital bed into what was Johnnie's dining room. He stayed there until November of 1944, again was put into the ambulance with me, and we went back to Provencal.

Mama and Elton were overjoyed to see us, and all the neighbors were so glad. One of them made my daddy a walker, something like a baby bed in shape. I am not an artist or I would try to draw it. It had wheels about six or eight inches on all four corners with a seat to sit on, if you got tired.

You could hold on to the railing and take two or three steps inside and back without moving the walker or stand up inside and push it through the door to the porch.

Papa walked again on January 1, 1945, with a cane, and lived another twenty-one years to enjoy life and his family.

He is said to have remarked that the tractor accident extended his life by ten years, as he would not have lasted twenty more years working hard on that sand hill farm at Provencal.

# ABOUT THE AUTHOR

Thomas Ard Sylvest was born in Provencal, Louisiana in Natchitoches Parish in 1925. He graduated from Provencal High School at the age of 16 and enrolled at Louisiana State University in 1942. He attended LSU for one year prior to entering the service during World War II. He served on Guam and Iwo Jima in the Army Air Corps as a member of the 302nd Fighter Control Squadron. After World War II, he returned to LSU and graduated with a degree in Agricultural Economics. Sylvest married Eloise Marie Therese Sobert on August 5, 1953 in Abbeville, Louisiana. They settled in Gramercy, Louisiana in 1968 and have lived there ever since. They have seven children, as well as multiple grandchildren and great-grandchildren.

Thomas Sylvest is the author of *Collard Greens: Growing up on a Subsistence Sandhill Farm during the Great Depression.*

# INDEX